A
POPE
LAUGHS

A
POPE
LAUGHS

STORIES OF JOHN XXIII

Collected by Kurt Klinger

Translated from the German by

Sally McDevitt Cunneen

Holt, Rinehart and Winston
New York   Chicago
San Francisco

For Marianne

Viribus unitis

CONTENTS

FOREWORD

*Let the words of my mouth
and the thought of my heart
find favor before you . . .*
PSALM 19:15

Nothing revealed the extraordinary humanity of "Papa Roncalli" more clearly than his purely spontaneous words and actions. If John XXIII departed from the text of an official address to lift his kind yet keenly perceptive eyes above the rim of his eyeglasses, all his listeners literally sharpened their ears to hear him. And in Rome, ears are sharp to begin with. They were sure to hear something congenial and humorous—but also something full of humility and inner greatness. Such remarks were typical of Pope John: frequently they were jokes, many times exquisitely ironic, often exuberantly cheerful. These extemporaneous comments were not oratorical or literary masterpieces—they were never meant to be that—but, rather, simple and affectionate words from one man to another.

This Pope knew how to reach and win the hearts of his fellow men. In his mass audiences, the eyes of his listeners brightened because they understood him; he did not preach at them, he spoke to them in homely words. His extemporaneous remarks were just as simple, yet they led more men to Christ and to prayer than all the sermons on hell-fire that have ever been delivered. Robert Schuman gave this description of Angelo Roncalli when the latter was about to leave Paris to become a Cardinal: "He is the only man in Paris in whose presence I feel a physical sensation of peace."

Paul VI gave evidence, only twenty-four hours after his election on June 21, 1963, that he would follow along the lines set by John's pontificate. But Papa Roncalli's successors cannot, however, take over or imitate his special gifts of character, his tone and style, or his affectionate gaiety. These qualities were well summed up in an article of October, 1959, in the London *Daily Express* which attempted to assess the achievements of the first year of John's pontificate. "The Pope must feel the deepest satisfaction with the achievements of his first twelve months on the papal throne. His prestige among the faithful is immense. His influence on the 'separated brethren,' the members of non-Catholic Christian churches, is greater than that of any previous pope. With the announcement that there would be a Second Vatican Council, he has given Catholic Christianity a great new inspiration. Beyond this, John XXIII is the first joyful Pope the Church has produced in a long time . . ."

After John XXIII's death, his Secretary, Loris Capovilla, wrote: "The Pope is not concerned with the accumulated resentments of the past. He is seeking to bridge contradictions and he is struggling for unity." Capovilla also remarked: "Pastor Roncalli is a joyful pope, who likes to laugh. This is a very rare attitude for someone sitting on the Chair of Peter." A high official of the Roman Curia, who served under both John XXIII and Pius XII, compared the two: "Pius XII was a great pope; John XXIII was a good pope. Pius XII was a great spirit; John XXIII had a great heart. The spirit convinces, but the heart conquers!" In his thinking, John himself always remained close to men. "The life of mankind," he said, "is a path to eternity, to heaven. One should follow it diligently so that blessedness may be unceasing."

His love of men had its roots deep in John's priestly soul, in his fatherly concern for his flock. He did not express this love to the faithful in complicated theological formulas which they would not have understood. On one occasion he explained his position in characteristically colloquial fashion. "I don't have liver trouble and my nerves don't bother me. I like to be around people." Neither this remark, which was so typical of Papa Roncalli, nor his jokes and frequent spontaneous remarks were ever printed by the Vatican newspaper *Osservatore Romano*. It was equally characteristic of John that through these omissions he allowed the paper to censor his remarks. But his imaginative sayings and the daily proofs of his sense of humor belong in a really faithful biography. Without them the image of John XXIII is incomplete. They made him the most popular pope in the history of the Church. Angelo Roncalli once commented ironically on the five biographies of his life which appeared simultaneously in January, 1959: "They are very fine and very interesting. But they are alike in one thing: they have nothing—or almost nothing—to do with me."

The spark he kindled has not been extinguished by his death. Hopefully, it will never be extinguished. It constituted, along with his motto "Bend, do not break," the essense of the Roncalli policy.

Those who did not understand Italian, however, missed many spontaneous pleasantries, a host of meaningful and extremely inventive stories, and the treasures of John's memory which revealed a rich experience of life. This—inevitably incomplete —collection of stories, episodes, and anecdotes has been assembled in an attempt to present a more rounded and hence truthful portrait of Angelo Roncalli. Although most are not recorded in any official or semi-official Vatican publication, they nevertheless belong to the story of John XXIII—the laughing Pope on the Chair of Peter—in much the same way that a sturdy pedestal forms an essential part of a noble monument.

A
POPE
LAUGHS

UNDERSTOOD

As a young priest, Angelo Roncalli was noted for his responsible editing of a diocesan newspaper, *La Vita Diocesana*, which he had helped to found. The paper was the official organ of the Bishop of Bergamo, and the masthead read: "Editor in chief, Reverend Doctor Guglielmo Carozzi; Editor, Don Angelo Roncalli." He had also worked on the respected *L'Eco di Bergamo*, which still exists.

In the first few weeks of his pontificate, John was irresistibly drawn to the editorial and printing offices of the Vatican newspaper, *Osservatore Romano*. He came unannounced, as he did so often in his tours of the Vatican. Neither Editor in Chief Raimondo Manzini, nor the assistant editors, nor any of the guides were there. This was quite satisfactory to the Pope.

The atmosphere of the place attracted him. To the specialist, printer's ink has a fascinating fragrance. The clicking and roaring of the presses seemed to carry him to higher regions, to make him feel powerful and free. For several minutes the Pope closed his eyes, listening to this booming rhythm as to a melody from his youth. Afterwards he asked for detailed explanations of modern improvements in the rotary presses and in printing techniques. The workers forgot their shyness, and with the encouragement of the Pope they began to speak with him almost as if he were a colleague.

John XXIII felt very much at home with journalists, too, and he often took the opportunity to see them. On January 27, 1963, he received the representatives of the Italian Catholic press. The Pope strongly urged his listeners to protest against immorality, especially against what he believed to be the constantly increasing lack of a moral sense in movies. Their protest must be sufficiently loud so that those in positions of responsibility could not ignore it. Above all, the various branches of the state should be encouraged to implement already existing laws in order to protect the young.

"Naturally, the press should always act in the service of truth." At this point John XXIII departed from his prepared talk. He told the journalists that they, too, were not above reproach, and that their sense of responsibility should force them daily to consider their choice of words with the utmost care.

"And if I permit myself here," continued Pope John extemporaneously, "to speak about the problems of the press in general and about those of journalists in particular, it is because I am not entirely a layman in this field. When I served as secretary to the Bishop of Bergamo, I wrote articles and editorials for local Catholic newspapers for almost five years. So I know—let us say, as a semi-practitioner, I know rather well that journalists often allow themselves little mistakes."

He did not mean that they exercised fraud, but that, more pardonably, they exercised a certain cleverness. The Pope used the word *difettuccio*, from *difetto* (defect, error), but the diminutive ending greatly tempers the strength of the word in Italian, making it a mild castigation, an imperfection rather than a willful fault.

This example reveals how very much at home one must be in Italian, as well as in one's native language, in order to be able to grasp Pope John's words, to convey their nuances, or what the Italians call the *sfumature* (shadings), in a meaningful translation. One can do justice to the spirit of John XXIII only by this complicated explanation of his *difettuccio*, not by a one-word translation. Instinctively the mind turns to the facile reporting of the journalist, a sharp contrast to the approach of the scholar. The journalist certainly records facts, but he makes them more available, if not more attractive, depending upon the audience addressed. In this regard, the Pope left the question open of whether he himself had occasionally made use of such a *difettuccio*, or if he was only remarking on the practice of his secular fellow editors who were present.

A CONFIDENTIAL LETTER

One shortcoming, or, if one prefers, a *difettuccio*, has been authenticated, at least in Angelo Giuseppe Roncalli's childhood. At the time, it preserved him from a sharp rebuke by a priest, but not from a forceful reprimand at home.

Angelino, as his mother still tenderly called him, was eight or nine years old when his parents, encouraged by their pastor and the local teacher, sent him to the fine episcopal college of Celano. It took Angelino about four hours daily to walk there and back. Often the boy returned to Sotto il Monte after dark, only to begin his studies tired and listless. He could expect no help from his parents, for they had never learned Latin.

Exhausted by the physical effort, he one day lost his ability to concentrate; he no longer wished to sit down at his books with his earlier zeal. His parents urged him in vain. Then they hit upon a way in which they could avoid giving him a good old-fashioned lecture; a friendly local priest could do it for them. Quickly the father wrote a letter and sent Angelino personally to deliver it to the priest. On the way, however, Angelino, suspecting something unpleasant, tore the envelope open, read the terrible contents, and ripped up the letter which asked the priest to give him a real scolding. He let the pieces of paper fly in all directions. The incident had a salutary effect on his whole life; never again did he need to be urged to study.

A GENTLE WINK

Compassion for ordinary people was one of Pope John XXIII's most prominent virtues. His social thinking, which had been formed in the humble home of his parents, was further developed at the side of Bishop Count Carlo Radini-Tedeschi, whom he had served as secretary in his youth; it became an inflexible moral demand which he maintained throughout all his life. The aristocratic Bishop had permanently engraved his name on the honor roll of the Italian Catholic labor movement because of his intervention on behalf of the basic rights of workers—indeed, the Bishop had once even led a strike himself.

The Pope did not look with favor on anyone who practiced self-serving class distinctions. He never lost an opportunity to remind those around him, "If anyone serve me, let him follow me; and where I am there also shall my servant be" (John 12:26).

During an audience in the spring of 1963, again he urged those who were well-to-do not to look upon their servants as a lower class of humanity, but to deal with them on terms of equality. Cardinals Cicognani, Urbani, Testa, and Di Jorio were present at the time. Pope John told them that he could remember very well how unpleasant it was to be slighted. In the rear of his Mercedes 300, for example, which had come installed with a single great thronelike seat, he had had a small chair added for his secretary.

"When I served as secretary to my bishop, I often had to run behind the noble man, because there was no room for me in the carriage."

With a roguish twinkle in his eyes, the Pope looked in the direction of the four cardinals.

"My *padrone* couldn't make any changes in his horse-drawn carriage. In the vehicles today, on the other hand, there's much more room . . ."

TEARS OF JOY

Natives of Bergamo stress the fact that their narrow land does not belong to Lombardy—although Italian maps often declare it does—but rather to Venice. The five hundred years in which the inhabitants of Bergamo lived under Venetian rule formed their character, which is quite different from that of the Milanese. The fact is that the Bergamese are gentler, more affectionate, and more understanding. Their exceptional love of music and of the plastic arts, as well as their religious fervor, are said to derive from their Etruscan ancestors. Students of Etruscan lore may possibly be right in comparing the sculpture on the sarcophagus of the corpulent Lord Magistrate Laris Pulenas in the Museum of Tarquinia (third to second centuries, B.C.) with a portrait of John XXIII.

With his subtle remarks, Pope John XXIII was a credit to all the Bergamese. At the same time, as a genuine son of the soil he was never lacking in frankness. Many times, in a friendly jest, he would soften a direct reference by speaking it swiftly in the Bergamese dialect, which is as rapid as it is difficult to understand. For example, only his relatives and friends from Sotto il Monte heard the words Don Angelo Giuseppe Roncalli spoke on August 10, 1904, when, newly ordained and recently graduated as a doctor of theology, he celebrated his first Mass in the parish church at home. In days to come there would be Masses to say in the Grotto of St. Peter's in Rome, at Florence, and in the Cathedral of Milan, but these would be anti-climactic after his first ceremony in his native village, in the presence of the entire Roncalli family.

After his first Mass was over, the young priest, proud but still unassuming, turned to the assembled congregation who were openly weeping with emotion. His own voice shook as he whispered, "Dear brothers"—then turning to his own brothers—"my dear real brothers, do not shed so many tears of joy! Seeing you cry like this makes me very sad."

WE ARE ALL BLIND

The new Pope had declared at his coronation, on November 4, 1958, that as a matter of policy "the new Pope would like above all else to help realize in himself that luminous image of the Good Shepherd which the Evangelist John has described for us. . . . In a special way this task of being a Good Shepherd to the flock lies close to our heart."

Immediately after the pontifical ceremonies in St. Peter's on Christmas Day, he was driven to the children's hospitals in Rome, *Bambino Gesu* and the *Santo Spirito*. Since the Vatican had not given much advance notice of this projected visit, it produced a stunned surprise; there was even general disbelief in the hospitals that the announcement was genuine. *Il Papa* was coming to visit the sick children? To comfort them and deliver his Christmas blessing in person? Such a thing had never happened before. The head physician at *Bambino Gesu* called the Vatican to check with the Secretary of State. It was true: the Pope was coming.

Scarcely had Pope John entered the first long corridor when cries and calls came from all the rooms: *"Papa, Papa, viene qui! Papa Giovanni una benedizione!"*

"Silenzio!" said the Pope in a loud voice, "I'll come to see all of you; just wait."

At the first bed, John inquired, "What is your name?" The little boy answered, "Angelo." "I was once named Angelo myself," replied the Pope, "but now they've given me another name." Another boy replied to a question about his age by saying that he was nine years old. The Pope said, "Well, I am really a few years older than you, but we both have the same father, the good God."

Among the patients soon to be released was twelve-year-old Silvio Colagrande, whose eyesight had been restored by a successful cornea transplantation. A dying priest, Don Gnocchi, had willed them to the youth. "I see you with Don Gnocchi's eyes," Silvio called out happily to the Pope. Beside him lay a boy who had accidentally sprinkled quicklime in his eyes while playing. The Pope spoke to him comfortingly, saying that he would hope to find a donor for him as well. "Men are not really wicked," he added.

Moved to tears, the Pope then walked to the bed of seven-year-old Carmine Gemma, who only three months earlier had lost his eyesight through a severe attack of meningitis. The otherwise strong little boy lay on his cot lifelessly. At the Pope's approach he called out, "You're the Pope, I know, but I can't see you."

John sat down on the side of his bed and for several minutes he stroked the child's pale hands in silence. After a while, almost as if he were talking to himself, he spoke: "We are all blind, sometimes."

CUT TO MEASURE

The decision in the conclave had just been made. The fifty-one cardinals present had chosen a new Pope on the eleventh ballot. Just outside the Sistine Chapel, the head tailor had prepared papal robes for five different prominent candidates. After his election, a pope may no longer wear red, but must appear only in papal white. While the throne is empty, the papal garments are made, following the estimates of the tailors and some sketches by the Cardinal Chamberlain.

In principle, the Cardinal Chamberlain, Benedetto Aloisi-Masella, would need to have the measurements of all the cardinals, including himself, since, during an interregnum, every cardinal is a potential pope. That would have actually meant preparing fifty-three different sets of Papal robes, one for each living cardinal. Such an estimate is purely theoretical, however, for only a few cardinals are *papabile*—that is, those with a serious chance of being elected. Cardinals Mindszenty (Budapest) and Stepinac (Belgrade) were not even present, since they had been unable to negotiate the right to leave their own countries.

When Pius XII was elected, there had been, in contrast, only three different likely candidates for the papacy. His robes, therefore, fitted him as if he had been poured into them. Besides, he had been Secretary of State.

The great uncertainty about Pius XII's successor is well documented by the fact that in the vacancy following his death, *Osservatore Romano* published twenty-five biographies of *papabili*, whereas it had printed only ten in the vacancy between Pius XI and Pius XII.

Of course, Cardinal Aloisi-Masella also kept in mind the facts of papal history. Since Hadrian VI, only Italians have occupied the Chair of Peter. But this practice is more than an expedient. The Italians maintain a nonpartisan standpoint on the Chair of Peter, as well as a certain attitude which predestines them— more, perhaps, than a stern German, a fiery Irishman, or a zealous American—to play the role of catalytic agents in the international Catholic world.

The Cardinal Chamberlain and the tailors, therefore, needed to make estimates only for the most likely Italian candidates. Contrary to tradition, Aloisi-Masella allowed five soutanes to be made up, to the measurements of Cardinals Agagianian, Ottaviani, Ciriaci, Ruffini, and Mimmi. As for Angelo Roncalli, who had emerged in the first rank of contenders only during the conclave itself, he could be fitted, if necessary, to the *corporis constitutio* of an Ottaviani or a Ciriaci, as could Aloisi-Masella himself.

Whose error it was, history may never be able to say. One of the tailors would have to tell us what went on in the workroom; there has been no report which would let us know what the tailors had against Roncalli. It was only after great difficulty, however, that they got the new Pope into the white soutane. While all those around him were murmuring a thousand apologies for the tight clothes, John said merrily, "Everyone wanted me to become Pope except the tailors!"

IN CHAINS

Napoleon is said to have frequently held his hands behind his back. Charlemagne kept his hidden beneath his mantle. St. Augustine used to clasp the cross. Eugenio Pacelli held his arms spread wide above his head, with the palms held toward the people. People said that Pacelli's hands were delicate and almost transparent.

The hands of John XXIII were almost the opposite of those of Pius XII. After Aleksei Adzhubei and his wife Rada, Premier Khrushchev's daughter, had been received in a special audience by the Pope on March 6, 1963, Mrs. Adzhubei spoke about John's hands: "He had hardly ascended the throne and raised his hands in a blessing when I was tempted to say to him that he had fine big peasant's hands, just like my father's. I saw the resemblance again very clearly when he handed Aleksei and me a pair of symbolic gifts, which were intended for my father, too, and he said: '. . . That's for your Papa.' "

The people of Rome were just as accustomed to the magnificent world-embracing sweep of Pius XII's blessing as were the inhabitants of the papal household. Disappointed faces appeared everywhere in St. Peter's Square when John XXIII began his first papal blessing, for he hardly raised his arms. His sign of the cross seemed to the Romans a pitiful gesture, for he appeared to be moving his wrist at about hip level.

Afterwards, when he had withdrawn behind the balcony, the Pope turned around with a helpless expression, explaining how little room for movement his soutane gave him. He had scarcely been able to raise his arms and hands in giving his blessing. "Look," he called laughingly to those standing nearby, "these are the chains of the pontificate."

A DOUBT

The tiresome process of being fitted into the ill-cut papal robes
was over. John XXIII climbed for the first time into the *Sedia
Gestatoria* to show himself to the faithful in his dignity as new
Supreme Pontiff. "Who knows," he whispered to his secretary, who had accompanied him to the balcony of St. Peter's,
as they looked at the surging crowd, "if all of those people
like me? After all, they didn't elect me."

HANDSOME?

The crowd had received Pope John XXIII's first blessing *Urbi et Orbi*. Vendors of ice cream, roasted chestnuts, and pious articles once more raised their voices bravely, praising their merchandise in the unique Roman idiom. Business was excellent. The people dispersed slowly, chattering and gossiping happily. "At last we have a pope again," was the remark heard most often and most clearly amid the continuous talk. For a moment the voice of one exuberant Roman matron rose above all the others. "He's not handsome," she cried, "but he does have a good heart!"

BREVIARY

Men learned very quickly that the primary concern of the newly elected Pope John XXIII was the care of souls, the genuine practice of Christianity. The ceremonies following the election were finally over; the first papal blessing had been given; the noise of the jubilant crowds began to fade away, and the long line of those offering congratulations came to an end.

The awareness that he alone was now to guide the Church had added to an understandable feeling of fatigue, and late in the evening of October 28, 1958, John went up to the papal apartments on the fourth floor of the apostolic palace. He had already given permission to have the seal to these rooms broken. According to ancient custom, the papal apartments are sealed when a pope dies, and only the new pope may break the seal. By tradition he is the first to enter the rooms, so that he can be the one to find and safeguard any valuable object left by his predecessor—possibly an unknown will. But Pius XII had died in his summer residence at Castel Gandolfo, and a thorough inspection of the Vatican apartments was quite unnecessary.

Now the papal chambers were filled with industrious commotion. Trunks and furnishings were being dragged across the floor, and servants and workmen were attempting to make the rooms habitable for their new occupant. The Pope hardly noticed the moving stream of people. He found a quiet corner and sat down; he pulled out his breviary and began to pray his office. He was discovered by his secretary, Monsignor Capovilla. The newly elected Pope looked up at him and smiled, quite undisturbed by the confusion around him: "Yes, dear friend, today's events made me fall behind in my office. I still have Vespers and Compline to finish."

DIZZY

It was not easy for John XXIII to become accustomed to the sedan chair, or *Sedia Gestatoria,* in which he was carried through great public gatherings. He understood, however, that it was necessary, in order that every pilgrim and believer, many of whom had made difficult journeys to Rome, might see the Pope clearly.

After one of his first mass audiences, John descended from the sedan chair and turned to the men who had been carrying him. He looked at the expensive and elaborately decorated throne he had just left and sighed, "The motion of that rocking chair makes me very dizzy."

LONELY

A few weeks after his coronation, Pope John confided to his secretary, Capovilla, that he was unable to sleep through the night any more. He felt lonely, and this kept him awake. He needed more conversation and more social stimulation to help him lose this feeling of being deserted. The secretary was silent. "Don't you think, Capovilla, that we might send for our good nuns from Bergamo?"

The little sisters were summoned. They not only took care of the Pope's household; they cooked for the entire papal court. They knew what the Pope liked to eat: simple, spicy foods. And their broad Bergamese dialect filled the apostolic palace with the conversation which the Pope had missed.

But he still found it difficult to spend certain hours alone. He simply could not accustom himself to the habit of eating all by himself, a practice which Pius XII had always maintained. In a very short time Capovilla was invited to join him at the table. The Pope's appetite improved immediately. Shortly afterwards he invited the cardinals of the Curia to be his table companions, one after the other. Little by little, bishops from all over the world, when they made their *ad limina* visits to Rome, were invited to join him for lunch or dinner.

Once a distinguished luncheon companion ventured to remind John of the solitary eating habits of Pius XII. "Well and good," John replied. "I value tradition and I grant that my predecessors did, too. I must confess, however, that I have never found any place in the Bible which suggests that the Pope should eat alone."

IDENTIFICATION PAPERS

Patriarch Roncalli had left Venice on the twelfth of October, 1958, in order to attend the conclave at Rome from which he emerged as Pope. He neglected to take along his personal identification papers; he did not even pack his will, which he was careful to keep with him on most occasions. The Patriarch told the Venetians when he departed that he hoped to be back in a few days.

On the twenty-ninth of October, John XXIII looked down from the window of the papal chambers on broad St. Peter's Square below. The conclave was ended. The Pope looked a little mournful as he watched one limousine after another carrying away the red-robed cardinals. Only twenty-four hours ago he had been a member of their college. With a sigh he turned around and murmured to the nearest bystanders: "Oh, I couldn't have gone back anyway; I don't have my identification papers."

NOBILITY

"Papa Roncalli" had scarcely ascended the papal throne when he was asked the traditional question: What title would his nearest relatives hold in the future? From antiquity, popes have had the right to adorn their relatives with grandiloquent titles. Simple people who were brothers, sisters, or nephews of a newly elected pope of humble origin could quite suddenly become counts and princes. Pacelli's three nephews—Carlo, Giulio, and Marcantonio—had inherited their titles: their father Francesco had received a hereditary title from the Italian King. The Pope can also place princely rooms in Vatican City at the disposal of his relatives, in which they can live rent-free and even hold court if they so desire.

The dignitary who had to approach John XXIII on this question knew that he would meet with a refusal or, rather, that John would not even understand the question. Nevertheless, tradition dictated that it must be asked, even though it was the protocol of an era long past. The master of ceremonies was very reluctant to approach the Pope. He tried to take courage from the memory of *Papa Sarto*, now St. Pius X, who came, like John, from peasant stock and who had declined the honor of making his sisters noblewomen.

John XXIII calmly indicated that his relatives should be called simply "Brothers and nephews of the Pope"—in other words, what they really were. "I believe that should be enough. And it seems to me that since they have expressed the wish to remain in their poor homes in Sotto il Monte, this is their greatest nobility."

SURPRISES

About three hundred thousand Romans, believers, tourists, and sightseers rejoiced when the name of the newly elected Pope was first announced: Angelo Giuseppe Roncalli, Patriarch of Venice. Then came the surprising papal name he had chosen: John XXIII. The crowd was even more pleased when the new Pope appeared on the balcony of St. Peter's and delivered his first blessing. St. Peter's Square was more brilliantly lit than usual. The additional floodlights were those of the Italian television company, RAI-TV, which had the honor of being the first television company to cover the proclamation of a pope and to beam it to the world.

The cardinals who had elected Roncalli on the eleventh ballot to be the successor of Pius XII now wanted to pack their trunks and get back to their homes and to their own dioceses. The Archbishop of New York, Francis Cardinal Spellman, had already booked an American-bound flight for that same evening. The ailing Cardinal Canali was in a hurry to return to his own quarters because of illness. Everywhere the noise of departure resounded. But John thought otherwise—not because he had become Pope and could not leave, but because he did not want to lose this extraordinary opportunity of consulting the illustrious experts about the Vatican in general and the papacy in particular. In short, when the Marshal of the Conclave, Prince Chigi, came to deliver a bunch of keys to the new Pope, John ordered the astounded man to close all the doors of the palace until the following morning. Instead of having trunks packed, John wanted a supper prepared for all the cardinals and conclavists.

During the genuinely friendly meal, the new Pope consulted each guest individually on Vatican customs. He was interested in all religious, political, economic, and social details. The cardinals were greatly surprised, for never before had a conclave continued after the election. At the supper, many of them became aware for the first time that the Pope they had chosen would be no transitional figure but would, instead, go his own way. The conversations at this historic supper ended without any formal comment by the Pope, but they laid the groundwork for many of his decisions which were to follow.

After a few weeks of the new pontificate, the papal secretary was asked how his boss was getting along in his new surroundings: "What's he up to?"

Capovilla gave an unexpected and laconic answer in the style of his superior: "What's he up to? Being Pope."

PP

Partito Popolare (Popular Party), founded by Don Luigi
Sturzo and Alcide De Gasperi after World War I before the
rise of Fascism, was the forerunner of the Christian Democratic Party of today. Almost every well-known postwar Italian Christian Democratic politician started as a member of the
earlier group. The open-minded and progressive wing of the
clergy, to which Angelo Roncalli belonged, welcomed the PP.
It was the first party in Italy which deserved the name
Catholic, and which permitted the political energies and abili-
ties of Catholics to develop. The originality of this initiative
can best be measured against the events of 1870, when the
thousand-year-old history of the Papal States had come to an
end. Pope Pius IX wanted to "punish" the new unified Italian
state, and his *non expedit* forbade Catholics to take part in
parliamentary elections either as voters or candidates.

The day after his election, John XXIII had to sign a number of documents. Before he wrote his papal name officially
for the first time, he practiced on scrap paper. Alone in his
study he energetically penned his new Latin signature. After a
few tries, he was satisfied. He had no sooner signed the first
official document than Secretary of State Tardini was announced. Delighted with the clear signature and the strong
and spirited line beneath, he showed Tardini his work. They
both looked at the sheet and read: Johannes XXIII PP
(*Papa Pontifex*). The Pope pointed to the two capitals and
murmured with wondering recognition to the confused Cardinal Secretary of State: *"Partito Popolare."*

[34]

RESOLUTION

For some time the Pope found it difficult to get dressed as quickly as usual because of his new and complicated papal garments. Every day he was late for his audiences, not only for public appearances but even for private receptions of distinguished visitors. Naturally enough, none of the court officials dared to say anything. On the other hand, it was a matter of concern—sometimes minor but often serious—to those in charge of protocol in the papal State Secretariat. They were especially concerned if a secular dignitary came to the Vatican for a private audience. Such visitors frequently had to wait a full hour.

Encouraged by the many reports of the new Pope's proverbial kindness, numerous ceremonial officials independently tried to influence the Secretary of State, Cardinal Tardini, to speak to His Holiness about his impolite tardiness. The task of nudging the precise Bergamese Roncalli was not altogether distasteful to the Roman Tardini. Romans are well known for their tendency to arrive late, while northern Italians—including the Bergamese—boast of their famous punctuality.

Tardini set about attaining his goal very prudently. "Holy Father," he said one day, "the Vatican, Rome itself, and especially Western diplomats are delighted that at last a punctual northerner sits on the Chair of Peter. Now there are no delays, such as there used to be; many times the heads of foreign nations had to wait a whole hour. Imagine, *Beatissimo Padre,* . . . what they must have told their governments!"

John grasped the point immediately. He looked up and interrupted Tardini in an equally sweet tone of voice: *"Ho già capito"* ("I understand"). "It doesn't matter to me," he explained, "what people think of me, if I am late or if I don't come at all. But I must always remain true to my own resolution: to be kind to everyone at all times."

PHOTOGRAPHY

In the year of John's coronation, Vatican authorities were besieged by requests from famous portrait photographers from all over the world who were anxious to photograph the new Pope. Only a few could be given permission. The Pope had an extremely heavy schedule which left little time for diversion. Just after he had finished sitting for one of these rare portraits, Bishop Fulton Sheen was announced. Still thinking of the photographs that had just been taken and anticipating the results, John greeted his visitor with the remark: "The good God has known for seventy-seven years that I would become Pope. Couldn't he have made me a little bit more photogenic?"

STAMPS

The first issue of Vatican stamps bearing Pope John's portrait was ready. The official in charge proudly laid the stamps before the Pope and ventured to suggest that the series was a very attractive and successful one. The Pope silenced him immediately: "Oh, come now, I know I'm not handsome, but I never thought I was *that* ugly."

THE INHERITANCE

After his coronation, John XXIII received all the important Vatican guests and foreign delegations in private or special audiences. Many photographs were taken of the magnificent ceremonies on these occasions. All authorized press photographers had to wear identity cards clearly visible on their lapels. They could then move about freely. But as the Pope entered or left, they had to stop taking photographs. Only Felici, photographer for the papal court, was permitted to move around with the papal party and shoot whatever and wherever he wished.

The house of Felici had received this privilege from St. Pius X. Every pope who succeeded him had renewed this extraordinary license. Felici is bound by it to deliver to the Papal See free of charge whatever photographs it requires. He is also obligated to supply the needs of the world press without payment.

Two Australian journalists who were traveling with the Archbishop of Sydney, Cardinal Norman Thomas Gilroy, spoke openly of their dissatisfaction with Felici. They had not found a single photograph showing their Cardinal with the new Pope. The court photographer, of course, could not possibly snap each cardinal at the precise moment of his encounter with the Pope.

Pope John heard of the dissatisfaction of the Australians with Felici in a special private audience. In a conciliatory tone, practically asking forgiveness for Felici, he said to them: "What can I do? I inherited him."

ABSENT-MINDED

During the nights following his election, Pope John XXIII was often unable to sleep. The immensity of the authority he had been given as visible head of five hundred million Catholics around the world brought him deep-rooted cares. He spoke of this later before a circle of visitors.

Many times he would scarcely fall asleep when some worry would seize him and wake him up again. One night when he was abruptly disturbed in slumber in this way, he mumbled: "I must talk this matter over with the Pope." After a short pause of realization he rubbed his eyes and spoke to himself again in a louder voice. "The Pope. . . ? *I'm* the Pope. Well, then, I'll have to talk it over with the good Lord."

THE THREE-DAY POPE

The Shah of Iran, Mohammed Riza Pahlavi, received the first audience given by John XXIII with all the Vatican ceremony reserved for royalty. A little later, thinking of such occasions and worn out by the mountain of papers to sign and the innumerable appointments he had to make, Pope John spoke of one of his predecessors who had died only three days after his election. "It's hard to believe," John concluded, "that he would have gone to so much trouble—just to be pope for three days!"

GALERO

In the first secret consistory held after his election, Pope John XXIII elevated twenty-three men to the rank of cardinal. This action created a sensation in Catholic and non-Catholic circles throughout the world. His predecessor, Pius XII, had not called such a consistory for many years. Moreover, and this was even more surprising, John XXIII had surpassed the limited number decreed by Sixtus V, who had declared that the Sacred College should consist of no more than seventy living cardinals. By adding twenty-three new cardinals to the fifty-three who were already of this rank, John had broken a tradition almost five hundred years old—abruptly and without long explanations.

At one point under Pope John, the college was increased to eighty-five. The demands of modern church leadership called for this number, John declared. And he added: "The letter should not kill the spirit."

The secret consistory, the assembly of all the cardinals who were staying in Rome, was traditionally held during the week of Ember days, either in Advent or Lent. This first consistory of John's pontificate was held on the fifteenth of December, 1958. It was followed, as usual, by a semi-public and then by a great public consistory. The high point of the ceremony in St. Peter's was the giving of the *galero*, when each new Prince of the Church received the tasselled red hat of a cardinal. After the splendid public consistory, the hat would never be worn again until the cardinal's funeral. The words spoken by the pope when he places the *galero* on each cardinal's head are significant: "Receive this red hat, the visible sign of your rank as a cardinal, for the greater glory of Almighty God and for the honor of the Apostolic See. May it signify your determination to stand up fearlessly, ready even to shed your own blood to strengthen your holy faith, for the peace and the security of your Christian people, and the protection and preservation of the Holy Roman Church."

Starting with Giovanni Battista Montini, now Pope Paul VI, John spoke these words of solemn moral responsibility to each cardinal in turn. The last was the French cardinal, André Jullien. As representative for all the others, he received a postscript to the official text from Pope John, who whispered in his ear: "And in the future, don't expect the red hat to do everything; let's use a little more brains and spirit . . . !"

PAPA GIOVANNI

In a very short time Romans began to call the new Pope John *Papa Giovanni.* Previously it had been forbidden to call a pope anything but his full title. Even *Papa Pio* for Pope Pius XII was frowned upon. For this reason Romans always said *Pio Dodicesimo* or even *il Santo Padre,* the Holy Father. But with John XXIII, the Curia, the priests, and the most traditional Romans all called him *Papa Giovanni* by common consent. Conditioned as they are to the presence of a pope among them, Romans can give no greater mark of distinction than a nickname.

On one of his walks around his worldly domain (one-sixth of a square mile), John XXIII entered unannounced into the workroom of Cardinal Gustavo Testa, like John himself from the province of Bergamo. In 1959, John had made him a cardinal and was later to appoint him Secretary of the Sacred Congregation for the Oriental Church. It had become traditional at such a visit to introduce one's most intimate co-workers to the Pope. "And here," interjected Cardinal Testa, "may I present to the Holy Father, Papa—Giovanni?"

"Who?" asked His Holiness in astonishment. "Papa, Giovanni?" Grins began to appear on all the faces in the group. "Yes," explained Cardinal Testa, "this worthy co-worker has Giovanni as his given name and Papa as his family name." (In business circles in Italy it is customary to give the last name first, and after that the given name.)

At length the Pope responded, "So, there are two *Papa Giovannis.* It doesn't matter. One Papa Giovanni would have been quite enough in Rome. But, anyway, since there are two, at least we'll work together."

WHISKY

During the conclave from which Angelo Roncalli emerged as John XXIII, television revealed for the first time to the entire world—radio and newspaper men had criticized the system earlier—that the smoke signal as a sign of papal election was more suitable to the Middle Ages than to the era of television and Telstar. The partly white, partly dark smoke confused even the Vatican radio announcers. They had to apologize frequently for their error. The column of smoke which rose from the chimney of the Sistine Chapel was first whitish, then definitely white, and only later definitely black.

It was amusing to observe in those days that the only whisky in popular demand in the bars, canteens, and restaurants of the Eternal City—even in the coffee bar at St. Peter's—was "Black and White."

Quite unknown to him, John soon made another Scotch whisky popular in Rome, a city which is usually unenthusiastic about whisky. His frequent excursions and walks through the streets of Rome gave him another nickname among the Romans: "Johnny Walker."

CHAMPION

During an audience for the members of the Administration of the Holy See's Possessions—actually the papal financial ministry—John XXIII was introduced to one of its members who had a very great number of children. "Well," he inquired affably of the distinguished dignitary, "how many children *do* you have?"

The answer was proudly given: "Fourteen, Holy Father. And, thanks be to God, they are all well."

"What?" asked the Pope. "Fourteen children and all in the best of health?"

The man, touched by his sympathetic interest, responded: "Yes, indeed, Holy Father, they are all in bouncing good health!"

Pope John looked at the thick-set man with the jovial face and exclaimed admiringly: *"Bravo*, fourteen times *bravo, bravissimo*—you have broken the record—you've beaten the twelve apostles!"

MINESTRONE

Everyone who lived in the Vatican realized after a few more of his visits to different parts of his domain that sooner or later John would visit the kitchen which took care of him and his closest co-workers. The Pope and his most immediate entourage were fed and served by five Italian Vincentian sisters, a congregation primarily dedicated to the service of the poor. They were quite unsophisticated in culinary affairs, and could certainly never be accused of spending money lavishly to stock the papal larder.

Suddenly one day the Pope decided to visit the kitchen when it was at the height of its activity, with kettles steaming and the odor of spices emerging from covered pots. At his entrance he paraphrased the words that Jesus spoke to Martha when he entered the house of the two sisters in Bethany: "Do not be anxious about your cooking! Think rather of your salvation."

One could see the genuine pleasure the double meaning of the remark gave him. The Vincentian sisters had obviously not gone to too much trouble about their cooking in the Vatican kitchen, although the Pope had a heartier appetite than his predecessors. In any case, the sisters had surely not neglected their spiritual welfare.

In order to be able to praise the hard-working women, Pope John walked up to the first kettle, lifted its cover and inhaled a little of the vapor rising from the boiling minestrone inside. "Hm, *buono!*" he declared. He took a spoonful that was offered to him and tasted a little. In the meantime the sisters made fervent invisible signs of the cross and quietly begged St. Martha for her intercession. It is not without reason that she has been made the patroness of housewives.

"Good soup," said John, in considered response to his sip, "really good." The tone was not quite convincing, but the sisters, encouraged, began to relax; they had expected the worst. "It just needs a little bit more spice," John added. "And sprinkle some more grated cheese on top, then it will be more appetizing and our customers will be happier."

EXAMPLE

The most recent predecessors of Pope John XXIII preferred to take their strolls in the Vatican gardens undisturbed. At most, they allowed one of their secretaries to accompany them. Just before the Pope appeared, always at a definite time, the gardeners and other workers on the grounds would withdraw.

But Pope John liked to take unannounced walks. The first time, all the workers were startled when they suddenly saw the Pope approach. Later, a fundamental change was adopted in this regard, as it was in many other practices. But this first encounter was a subject of amusement to the Pope. A group of street cleaners took to flight as if they were retreating from a leper. Each man tried to hide, some behind bushes, others behind a projecting wall.

The Pope did not enjoy this game of hide-and-seek. "Come out again, all of you," he called out. "I won't do anything to you. I want to talk to you. Come. Hurry up, *avanti, venite!*" Timidly, and very slowly, one after another, they came up to the Pope. He did not let them stay on their knees very long, but instead asked them about their families. After they had all had the chance to boast that they were the fathers of a fairly large number of children, John said, "There were twelve children in our home, too. They are all farmers except myself. Five of them are still living." Then the Pope wanted to know what they received as wages for their work. "What?" he replied, frowning, when they told him that they made only 1,000 lire a day ($1.60). "That's only 24,000 lire a month [$38.40]. No family with lots of children can live on that. What has become of justice? Just wait, we'll change that."

The Pope turned around and went immediately to his study to investigate. First he canceled the contract with the Roman firm which, in a written agreement for the cleaning and maintenance of Vatican streets also stipulated the small salaries given the workers. Considering the fees mentioned in the contract, the company certainly should have been able to pay higher wages.

This marked the beginning of a general review of all wage and salary scales in the Vatican. The lowest wages were doubled, while the higher ones were increased in a gradually decreasing scale, so that today the wages and salaries in the Vatican are significantly higher than those in the rest of Italy. At the same time, the Pope ordered that for each child a man had, he should receive an extra monthly allowance of 10,000 lira. It is not surprising that Roman workers now compete for jobs in the Vatican, which only recently they scorned.

When the Pope announced these decrees, affecting almost three thousand salaried workers in the Vatican, he counseled their administrators in these words: "We cannot always require others to observe the Church's teaching on social justice if we do not apply it in our own domain. The Church must take the lead in social justice by its own good example."

APPRENTICE

Pope John found it very difficult to get used to some things required by Vatican protocol. For a long time he said "I" instead of "We" in his official talks. Popes are expected to use the royal "We," at least on official occasions. The hard task of being forced to use this form of address had come to him suddenly, and it frightened him a little. One day he looked through his slightly open door and saw a large number of visitors gathered in the antechamber. He braced himself, opened the door, and called out to the astonished group that they should please wait patiently just a little longer: *"Dio Mio!* So many people! Give me some time to learn the business of being Pope: Let me practice a little first!"

MODERATION

It was during a general audience in St. Peter's Basilica on December 17, 1958, that Pope John XXIII greeted the faithful and many pilgrims from all over the world in German and in English for the first time. After he had spoken in Italian and then in French, he asked pardon of the crowd that he had not yet learned German and English well enough to be able to address his visitors in these languages, too. He asked them to be patient and wait until he had improved in his studies of these tongues. The Pope used a well-known Italian saying which originated among farmers, and conveys the thought, "Good things take time" (*Campa cavallo che l'erba cresce*).

As it happened, John delivered holiday greetings in the two languages at Easter and Christmas only. The ability to give major addresses in these tongues seemed to be beyond him, despite his public promise to his visitors from German- and English-speaking countries that he would speak in their language on their next visit. Moreover, the Pope concluded that it would be a good idea not to talk quite so much, for it is easy to burn one's tongue. For this reason, he said, he would recommend moderation. "Tongues seem to grow in the way men ordinarily use them—pointedly."

HEAVYWEIGHT

Papa Roncalli came from such a modest home that he had a deep distaste for pomp. Only on really ceremonial occasions, for example, did he make use of the *Sedia Gestatoria*, the papal sedan chair. The *sediari*, the twelve men in scarlet silk and velvet that bear the throne aloft, were called upon far less frequently by John XXIII than by Pius XII. John often went to St. Peter's on foot.

His social sense always brought him close to those in need, to the poor. He was constantly concerned for the welfare of others. It was inevitable, therefore, that one day shortly after his coronation as pope, when the *sediari* had performed their office for him several times, that he should have inquired about their wages. The papal court was dumbfounded, for this kind of interest in Vatican affairs was not customary in the previous pontificate. "Why does the Holy Father concern himself with such a *bazzecola* [trifle]?" he was asked by a subordinate. John XXIII looked at the man, then stared into the distance for a moment. It was almost as if he were envisioning the ethereal figure of his predecessor. Then he explained: "They should receive a bonus to compensate them for the increase in papal weight."

PEASANT

An earthy aroma pervaded St. Peter's—an unusual rural at-mosphere reigned in this imposing house of God. Strong, solid peasant heads on thick-set and partly bent shoulders circled John XXIII in a special audience for Italian peasants and small agricultural landholders. The men held their broad-brimmed straw hats in their hands. About ten thousand of these farm workers had come to Rome. They were dressed in their Sun-day best, of course, men and women, girls and boys, but their dark clothes, mostly of homespun wool, bore with them the fragrance of their native soil. Most of the men walked clumsily in their unaccustomed white shirts, collars and ties, shifting from one foot to another. Thoughtful and fervent, the women and girls looked around the Basilica in astonishment, quite unlike the sophisticated Romans, and they seemed ill at ease in the vast dimensions of the giant building.

Pope John sensed the uncertainty in the ranks of his visi-tors, and he was even more aware of their embarrassment. With one sincere remark, however, he was able to put them at their ease, restore their courage, and almost transform the polished marble floor into the solid, familiar fields of home.

"I know," said the Pope, "how unrewarding work on the land can be. I speak to you as the son of Roncalli the wine-grower. And yet, if the good Lord had not made me a pope, I would rather be a farmer than anything else."

A lively burst of laughter was his reward.

JAILERS

Protocol does not always permit the Pope to mingle with the crowd. Especially in mass audiences in St. Peter's Basilica the rush of spectators can become so powerful that the Swiss guards and the police must become almost violent to hold back unruly men and women. In particularly critical situations the Chamberlain and other high ecclesiastical dignitaries have to surround the Pope and ward off the crowd in order to prevent his being crushed. Pope John used to use a phrase in these situations to indicate his unity with the faithful, "Here they come again, my jailers!"

FAMILY AUDIENCE

A few days after his coronation John held a special audience for his family, a privilege granted to each new occupant of St. Peter's Chair. The Roncallis entered the apartments in the apostolic palace timidly. The splendor of the place troubled their simple souls. Finally, bashful and confused, they stood before the white-clad figure of the Pope. In their confusion they dropped their little presents. Peasant bread, ham, and wine, packed in brightly colored handkerchiefs, all tumbled to the floor. John looked at their staring eyes and open mouths. Although the comedy of the situation did not escape him, he spoke reassuringly: "Don't be afraid. It's only me."

CANARY GERMAN

After his coronation, Pope John spoke to his closest collaborators about the difficult inheritance Pius XII had left behind
him. The Pope spent hours, days, and even weeks reading and
organizing the notes which Pius XII had left. One afternoon
his co-workers entered his library while he zealously pursued
his languge studies. They knew that Pope John—like his predecessors—preferred to address the faithful in their own native
languages, and they were not surprised to find him freshening
up his study of languages he had learned earlier. They had not
observed him studying new languages, however. They were
all the more surprised, therefore, when in answer to their
question as to what language he was working on, John replied, "German. Yes, I'm learning German now," he said, "although I must confess I find it very difficult. But that's the only
language the *canarini* [canaries] understand, the ones Pius
XII left me. And this is still the easiest part of a difficult inheritance."

THE DRUM

John XXIII wanted to make the acquaintance of everyone who worked for him, either directly or indirectly, or at least to speak to them. After his coronation he scheduled regular audiences for all the different groups of people working for the Holy See. In May, 1959, it was the turn of the "armed forces." Besides the noble guard, the Swiss guard, and the Palatine guard of honor (also called the palace guard), these forces included the papal police force, which served both as an actual police force and also as a corps of plain-clothes men trained in criminal matters.

One group after another passed in review before the Pope, each man calling out his name, rank, and station in a loud, clear voice. There were almost five hundred genuflections, since, in the presence of the Pope, it would be improper to stand rigidly at attention.

At one point it was the turn of the drummer of the Palatine guard band, who carried before him not only his drum but an imposing paunch. As the man genuflected, kissed the Fisherman's ring, and then rose to his feet, the Pope stared at the corpulent figure before him. With a compassionate smile he began to tease him gently: "One can see that things are going well with you, so there's no need for me to ask how you are, as I did the others. The sound of all that drumming seems to have expanded you. But don't let that bother you—people always listen to us fat men!"

To the great amusement of the Pontiff, the sergeant-drummer replied in a similarly bantering tone: "Holy Father, grease makes us gracious!"

MODEL PUPIL

John XXIII tried to show some mark of attention to every visitor who attended one of his private audiences. Besides a gift, as a souvenir of the occasion, he tried whenever possible to speak a personal word that the guest would know was directed to him alone. In Italian and French, Bulgarian, Greek, Turkish, and Russian, the Pope could always find something pertinent to say: a proverb, a word of encouragement, something more than a merely polite remark.

When former President Dwight D. Eisenhower walked into the Pope's private library on December 6, 1959, however, John appeared a little disconcerted. His spoken English was not exactly the kind taught at Oxford. But he was anxious that "Ike" should know that he had prepared for this encounter. On the other hand, Ike had not worn the morning coat Vatican protocol indicated, which naturally did not disturb John, especially because the visit was classified as an informal one, and was not the kind usually accorded to heads of state. (British Prime Minister Harold Macmillan took Ike's cue. When Macmillan appeared for a private audience on November 23, 1960, he, too, appeared without a morning coat.)

Because of his lack of proficiency in English, John used the language only for the beginning and the end of his greeting, most of which was delivered in French. He addressed "The President and the noble American people." He also said, "Dear Mister President, Your Excellency," and at the end of his talk he concluded, "God bless you all."

Eisenhower was touched, and after an exchange of gifts he thanked the Pope for his linguistic consideration: "Your Holiness speaks English well." With disarming irony the Pope replied in Italian, "I'm going to night school. But I'm not doing very well. . . . I'm always at the bottom of the class."

ATHEIST

When John XXIII moved to his summer residence at Castel Gandolfo for the first time, he received the city fathers in an audience, as his predecessors had always done before him. Among them were several Communists. John enjoyed himself thoroughly with the Communists; one might have thought they were his own brothers. They had intended to inform the Pope about the little community: how badly the rich treated the poor, how inadequate the subsidies of the provincial government were to alleviate the situation, and so forth. But they never got around to it. The Pope inquired so sincerely about their own personal lives that they forgot their complaints. Encouraged and comforted, they left his residence to join the crowd in the square before the balcony which had been waiting for John XXIII to appear and give them his blessing.

The shouts of *Viva* seemed endless. One of the best-known Communists, who had been among those speaking to the Pope, shouted and clapped his hands with the loudest. "Why?" a neighbor wanted to know. "Why are you yelling so loudly? You're an atheist, a Communist!"

The man replied excitedly, with tears in his eyes and trembling lips, "He's the son of a worker. He knows what manual labor is. I'm clapping for a poor man of the people who has been made Pope."

SOLIDARITY

On December 26, 1958, when John had been Bishop of Rome for almost two months, he surprised everyone by his visit to the immense Roman prison of *Regina Coeli* (Queen of Heaven). The Romans could not remember when a pope had last exercised his pastoral function as Bishop of Rome by visiting the men who were in prison.

The prison authorities did not consider it suitable to make the somber atmosphere more cheerful by introducing tapestries, murals, or drapes. One assistant warden, however, had seriously suggested decorating the great dining room in which the Pope would bestow his blessing on the prisoners so that it would resemble a Roman basilica on a great feast day.

Above all, Pope John brought the prisoners hope. "My dear sons, my dear brothers," he said in an impromptu talk which was almost more like a confession. The men listened intently, in absolute silence. Long before his urgent plea that in the future they should not stray from the right path again, with the wink of an accomplice he confided to these guests of the Queen of Heaven that he himself had once been a thief. Before he told that story, however, he disgressed by telling one about a relative of his who had gone hunting without a license and had been promptly caught and thrown in jail.

"Go ahead and laugh, today I am your prisoner." Then came the confession: "When I was a boy I stole something once; it was an apple. My feelings of remorse were just as great as yours, and for a long time I repented for my sin. But I was lucky; I was not caught!" In the pause that followed, an infectious smile spread across the Pope's countenance, and he concluded in the Bergamese dialect: "How could I have given the apple back anyway? I had eaten it a long time ago!"

NO STOPPING

"It's incredible," said a motorcycle policeman, "you just can't stop this Pope. He's constantly on the move. I never have a peaceful minute any more. My spaghetti is always cold when I get home." He was complaining to his colleagues who, like him, had been assigned by the Roman chief of police to be a part of the Pope's motorcycle escort. It did, in fact, often happen that the Pope would make an unannounced trip at the last minute, and then the motorcycle escort had to drop everything and rush to the Vatican.

"No wonder," remarked another policeman dryly, "just look at that traffic sign in front of the bronze door of the Vatican, the one that used to be only for the Pope. It says, very plainly: 'No Stopping!' "

FALDERAL

The atmosphere of the Vatican was completely altered under Papa Giovanni. From the beginning, John directed the change toward a greater simplicity and naturalness. He started with the Vatican newspaper *Osservatore Romano*. The rather pompous speech of the Curia and the long, involved sentence-structure used at the Vatican were the first to go. He let the editors of the distinguished Vatican paper know that in the future when they were referring to the Pope, they should not call him "our spiritual ruler." They should not employ inflated phrases, such as "the chosen one in his inspired and sublime discourse," but should simply state, "The Pope said." They were also asked to eliminate the introductory sentence—"We present the following speech as we have gathered it from his august lips." Such wording was not only stuffily old-fashioned, it was ridiculous.

When John looked through the sheaf of telegrams which his State Secretariat had composed to thank all the dignitaries who had sent congratulations after his coronation, the Pope was genuinely shocked at their unctious style. "Fronzoli, Fronzoli," he called out. "This is all nonsense and falderal. Leave out these superfluous ornaments. Be simpler and warmer. At least try!"

SPIRITUAL EXERCISES

The Holy See contains a large automobile park. Many automobile manufacturers have presented the popes with their best models. French and English firms constantly compete with Italian manufacturers in this regard. After ascending the papal throne, each new pope is regularly presented with a luxury limousine from the United States as a sign of national homage. American Catholics pay the bill for these leviathans of the road.

Pope John XXIII, however, traveled only in a Mercedes-Benz, as does his successor, Paul VI. When the designers were planning the special car for the Bishop of Rome, they took into consideration the fact that protocol would often oblige him to travel in his official robes. The necessity of bending and stooping makes entering and leaving the vehicle very difficult and uncomfortable under these circumstances. A special device was therefore added to the Pope's Mercedes 300 which permitted the roof to disappear automatically. An almost invisible extra foot pedal was placed on the floor near the driver's foot to control the silent mechanism. This movable roof permitted the Pope to rise even when wearing a tiara (when he had to), or when wearing a mitre and his full official robes. He did not need to bend or even to be careful getting in and out, and he could also bless the crowd while standing up inside the car.

But before he became used to it, the Pope would not always wait the few seconds necessary for the roof to open fully. John XXIII was so eager to get out when he reached the end of the trip and saw the faithful as well as local officials already on their knees that he would inevitably bump his head on the moving roof. Although he was quite annoyed, he never blamed himself or the roof. He had too much respect for the precision of the electrical mechanism. The papal anger came to rest instead on the driver, along with the hint that he always pushed the pedal too late. The chauffeur accepted these reprimands with resignation, knowing that John was not usually strict. Besides, Papa Roncalli did not know how to be really insulting.

Once, after he had bumped his head again in this fashion, the Pope gave his driver an ultimatum: "In the future, Guido, make up your mind whether you are going to open the thing or let it remain shut, and then give me the proper signal. You may amuse yourself with it when I am not in the car. But as for these jigglings of yours, I must say that I cannot call them spiritual exercises."

A LIFE OF SACRIFICE

The territory over which the Pope has jurisdiction as Bishop of Rome is very broad, stretching in a wide arc from the sea to the Albani and Tiburtine Mountains. It contains almost three million inhabitants at the present time, and the city of Rome is constantly growing. Church officials are anxious to keep in step with civil authorities, who envision a population of ten million in the year 2,000, according to the most recent projections. Under John XXIII, ecclesiastical authorities responsible to the Roman General Vicariat were given strong encouragement to plan new churches, as well as future Church welfare centers for the distribution of material aid and institutes for the education of children and adults.

In the course of his visits outside the walls of the Vatican, especially during the season of Lent, the Pope used to gather detailed information about the lives of the people who lived in the poorest and most thickly populated sections of the city. Almost every day, illegal huts made of corrugated iron are secretly put up in these neighborhoods. Usually they are assembled so speedily that the police arrive on the spot too late to prevent their erection. Nothing stops a policeman from driving his jeep slowly, of course, and a humane Italian rule states that these huts cannot be torn down once the roof is up. On the other hand, a commando police force must intervene to prevent the start of such construction, even if their only tip is from an anonymous telephone call.

The sections of Rome which are filled with these corrugated huts and caves naturally spoil the appearance of the city, especially since they flank the great and venerable consular streets. Their number persistently increases in Tiburtino, Salario, Primavalle, Prenestino, Quarticciolo, Tufello, and Cinecittà, districts that almost all have beautiful names with Virgilian resonance—but only to non-Italians. To the modern Roman they mean the districts populated by the *abusivi*—trespassers who have illegally erected a roof over their heads.

Pope John was not concerned with this bureaucratic anger. As pastor of this poor flock, he felt bound by charity toward them. He sought to win the hearts of these abandoned people so that he might help them to help themselves. He used to call the area "My personal mission territory," knowing very well that it was a "tough neighborhood" which regularly voted Communist.

Every year John visited this quarter during Lent. Numerous petitions in bad handwriting were pressed upon him at every visit. He took them all. Every one requested the same things: a decent home, work, and food suitable for human consumption.

On one of these visits John asked a twelve-year-old boy his name. "Giovanni," the boy said. "A good name," the Pope replied. "I'm called Giovanni, too."

The Pope inquired further: "What do you want to be when you grow up?" "Pope, like you," replied the boy promptly, to the amusement of everyone, especially the Pope, although the laughter of the Vatican functionaries seemed a little strained.

John XXIII laid his heavy peasant hand on the boy's frail shoulders and whispered to him, just loud enough so that a few bystanders could hear him: "You've chosen a difficult voca-tion. It is—you can believe me—a life of sacrifice."

FELICI

"Caro Tardini, please, I beg you not to keep throwing confusion in the ranks."

The Pope's parents, Giovanni Battista Roncalli and Marianna, nee Mazzola.

The Pope's birthplace in Sotto il Monte.

Dom Angelo Roncalli as a twenty-year-old priest.

Richard Cardinal Cushing kisses Pope John's ring, as Gregory Cardinal
Agagianian looks on.

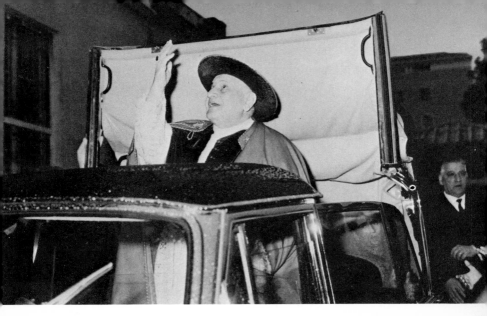

The Mercedes with the movable roof.

With President Eisenhower, Lt. Col. Vernon Walters, the President's official interpreter, and Barbara Eisenhower, his daughter-in-law.

Pope John gives a medal and a rosary to seven-year-old Katherine Hudson, of Oklahoma City, Oklahoma.

The children's hospital (*Bambino Gesu*) in Rome.

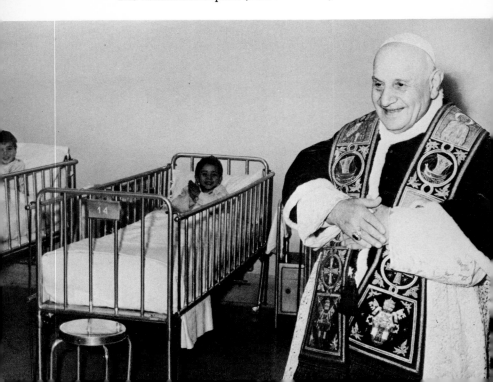

Pope John about to embrace The Most Rev. Poreku Dery
after consecrating him bishop of Wa, Ghana.

On a stone bench in the Vatican gardens.

FEAR OF THUNDER

"Did you hear the thunder last night?" Pope John inquired of his surprised visitors at an audience on November 13, 1959. He was receiving the spiritual counselors of the Catholic Women's League of Italy, and the audience was primarily composed of women. Before he began his prepared address, he recalled the unusually violent thunderstorm of the preceding night. "Dear God, what a storm. What powerful thunder and lightning." (Hundreds of trees had been uprooted during the night, fires were started by the lightning, roofs were blown off, and numerous accidents had occurred on the streets of Rome. The firemen had been forced to respond to at least five hundred alarms.) "Believe me, my dear fellow citizens, the Pope was afraid, too. I jumped out of bed and started to pray. I chanted the Litany of the Saints and only then did my fear begin to diminish. At last I was able to get back to sleep, and this time my dreams were edifying."

SECURITY

The crisis with Cuba had reached its dramatic climax, and the appeal made by the Pope to the participants appeared to have had some effect. The bitter chalice had by-passed mankind. But not all the dark clouds were gone; the threat of war still continued.

At this point John XXIII spoke to a mass audience of the faithful in St. Peter's: "Here you are safe. No cannon will be shot; we have no atomic bombs."

In his next mass audience he departed again from his original speech. He had been talking fervently of the living Church, which has always and everywhere welcomed, demanded, and supported every advance toward the peace, security, freedom, and the well-being of mankind. He then addressed the crowd spontaneously: "Now you are here in St. Peter's Basilica, and it does not seem to me that you find yourselves in a clinic or a hospital. No, the Church of the Lord, the Church of Jesus Christ is not dead. Or do you think that what you see around you are the sick and the dying?"

A PURE CONSCIENCE

During the interval when the Romans were still astonished at the new Pope's activities, John visited the Benedictine Abbey of Subiaco south of Rome. This abbey, called "nullius," is directly dependent on the Holy See, and has always been highly esteemed both by the popes and by secular princes. With St. Scholastica, it is one of the dozen famous monasteries in the Subiaco area, the birthplace of the Benedictine order. St. Benedict lived here in retreat for three years, beginning when he was fourteen. Here is the cave in which pious tradition states that St. Benedict was fed by a raven. In the abbey, consecrated to St. Scholastica by the Abbot Stephen after its reconstruction in 705, the first books printed in Italian were produced by two Germans in 1464. The monastery of St. Benedict is one of the most remarkable religious and artistic treasures on the Apennine Peninsula. It contains two churches, one above the other, as well as several grottoes and chapels.

John was received by the community and its abbot in the spacious upper church.

Subiaco was festive with decorations. A great number of people, especially young ones, had been attracted to Subiaco for this visit, which was the first of its kind since the reign of Pius IX. Before those in charge realized what was happening, some boys had clambered up onto the precious carved antique choir stall to get a better view of the Pope. While they were shuffling about the benches in their dirty shoes, the sacristans, who were disturbed, began to chase the boys out, but their efforts were interrupted by the commanding voice of the Pope: "Leave them alone, let them stay there. Their *conscience* is still quite pure."

SOCIAL JUSTICE

When John XXIII announced his intention to write a new social encyclical, some of his closest collaborators suggested that it might not be necessary to treat themes which had already been so fully explored by his predecessors. They were referring to the Encyclicals *Rerum Novarum*, of Leo XIII, and *Quadrigesimo Anno*, of Pius XI. Surely these had clarified and defined the Church's position once and for all on the theme of social justice and her unmistakable support of the workers' welfare. "No," said John, "many years have passed since they were written. The world travels faster than we do. We must adapt daily and totally so that we do not limp along behind. Otherwise we will be outrun. By whom? I leave that to you to figure out."

MAY DEVOTION

Every year in the month of May, John XXIII asked the faithful to pray the rosary with special fervor, since that prayer had been so suitably chosen to honor Mary. In the last mass audience he held before his death, on the first Wednesday in May, 1963, Pope John added an impromptu appeal to the faithful: "I know it is often very hard to pray the rosary devoutly. But you ought to set aside a little time for it each day. I have no objection to your missing it if you have urgent work, or some danger which is threatening you, or an important family matter you cannot put off. But it is mostly laziness which makes us neglect the rosary. Later in old age, when we have learned its importance, we recite it more willingly, because it comforts us and gives us strength and hope. But even when we are young we ought to love it. Unfortunately, I must confess that as a boy, I, too, neglected it; I much preferred running around outside to staying at home saying the rosary."

EYEGLASSES

John was farsighted; for reading and writing he needed to wear glasses. He was often forced by the pressure of his obligations to lay aside letters he had begun and, of course, to remove his glasses when he did. When he needed them again a short time later, however, he frequently could not find them. The Pope Roncalli was not infallible in regard to this habitual weakness of people who wear eyeglasses. His secretary, the Master of Ceremonies, and his bodyguard all learned to carry an extra pair of glasses so as to assist the Pope in an emergency.

During the solemn opening of the Second Vatican Council in St. Peter's Basilica, the Pope once again could not find his glasses. When he came to the part which referred to the missing bishops, "noticeable here today by their absence, because they are imprisoned for their faithfulness to Christ," the Pope began to search in his robes for his eyeglasses, obviously without success. But he did not lose himself as he had the glasses. After a short sigh he spoke: "If your eyesight fails, there's nothing you can do about it. That is *God's* will. But misplacing my glasses—that's sloppiness on *my* part."

APPLAUSE

John XXIII waged constant war against the loud approval he met from his fellow countrymen in church. Despite his love of people, he did not like to be applauded in church. As a son of northern Italy, where moderation in all things is admired, he preferred the quiet devotion practiced there. He thought that every noise—shouts of joy as well as clapping—should stop at the church door. Whoever enters into the house of God should conduct himself reverently and observe a respectful silence.

The Romans, however—and almost all southern Italians— love noise. Silent affection seems disrespectful to them. The fact that they show their enthusiasm in a boisterous way is not merely a matter of temperament; it is an expression of their own ardent life which cannot be checked. The Pope never admonished them publicly, despite his own tendencies.

Once early in his pontificate, John exercised indirect pressure. The invitations to a solemn ceremony at St. Peter's sent out by the Head Chamberlain announced that the Pope would not be carried on the *Sedia Gestatoria*, but would, instead, walk to the Basilica. Because it was a funeral service, there should be no applause when the Holy Father appeared. For the first time absolute silence reigned when the Pope was seen. But on all sides one heard the remark, *Però è un pó triste* ("It's a little sad").

After this episode the Head Chamberlain no longer tried to exercise his influence, but the Pope did not relax. Soon after this successful but unpopular enforcement of silence, he tried for the first time in his own way. "I am happy to see so many pilgrims and members of the faithful before me. Don't stop coming to visit me, but please, be considerate. A pilgrimage should be edifying. Try to maintain greater silence." This was the first of a series of improvised talks which John gave to his mass audiences. It was held in the Basilica, with the papal throne directly in front of St. Peter's tomb. "Especially here, where the prince of the Apostles has found his last resting place, you should be quiet." With a sigh he concluded: "I often wonder how poor St. Peter can rest down there with all the racket you make up here."

On another occasion the Pope cited Scripture, but he still did not produce the desired results. "By waiting and by calm you shall be saved, in quiet and in trust your strength lies" (Is. 30:15). But Romans want to greet their pope with a rousing welcome wherever he appears.

As had been his custom every year, in Lent of 1963 the Pope went to Mass in a different parish church in Rome each week. Over a million people assembled on these six Sundays, including a very large number of young people, and lined the streets to see the Pope, to show him their respect, to receive his blessing—and, naturally, to cheer him loudly in church.

On Sunday, March 3, 1963, John XXIII drove to a heavily populated quarter in the southeastern section of the Italian capital. More than 150,000 worshipers, sightseers, and children crowded the streets around the church in the Quarticciolo district. The Mercedes 300 slowly made its way through the throng. Little girls with shrill voices shouted to policemen: "Don't stand there staring; take us up on your shoulders. We want to see the Holy Father once ourselves." Often they were obeyed, but not always. The bravest boys in the district hung from the trees like bunches of grapes. Orphans in uniform waved paper flags bearing the Vatican colors—white and yellow. Loudspeakers broadcast records of pious music. Women signaled each other with pocket handkerchiefs and shrieked with excitement over the Pope's visit.

Inside the church the *Credo* sung by the choir was drowned out by the joyous shout *Viva il Papa* from below. At the *vexilla regis* the noise grew even louder. A loud-speaker intoned a reminder to be quiet: "Attention, the Holy Father is now incensing the relic of the holy cross." Silence did not follow, how-

[72]

ever; on the contrary. Only when Bishop Cunial blessed the crowd with the relic did they subside into a devout silence.

Outside, the waves of sound continued to rise and fall. Immediately after the blessing, when the Pope began to speak from the altar, the enthusiasm of the crowd increased in volume once more. John XXIII talked on undisturbed. The people calmed down a little so that only a murmuring remained, and the Pope took the opportunity to say: "If we want to understand each other, when I speak you will have to restrain your tongues a little. After all, I made the long trip so that *I* could speak to you here, and now *you* chatter incessantly. Just wait. If I cannot speak, I will drive away again. Bite your tongues if you want to satisfy your hearts."

Several priests were at their wits' end. All hushings and appeals for silence were fruitless; John was able to deliver only half of his address. The waves of enthusiasm made any further words impossible.

The Pope, full of understanding, did not give up, but called out cheerfully to the crowd a line from Psalm 88, "Happy the people who know the joyful shout."

On Passion Sunday the Pope was firmer with the crowd when they greeted him with loud applause as he entered St. Basil's Church: "There should be no clapping in church, not even for the Pope." His sudden and quite unusual severity momentarily stunned the crowd, which was largely composed of working people. But as soon as the Pope's good-natured smile returned, the applause resumed and the shouts of joy almost shook the walls of the church. John wanted to speak again, but because of the tumult he found it impossible. He resorted to his final weapon; he turned to go. For the first time the crowd was silent. They listened reverently to a talk which was an indirect reply to all the critics who had hurled at John XXIII the charge that he was "too far to the left." This remark had been made with special insistence after his private audience with Khrushchev's son-in-law.

"The Pope is always an optimist," he told them. "He sees nothing but good. I am the echo of the words spoken by Jesus, who wanted the welfare of all and harm for none. I prefer a 'Yes' to a 'No.' See—the Pope arms no nation. He has no threatening rockets, no armored divisions. He conducts no politics and is not involved in big business. I am a child of workers who has lived among the people, and I intend to remain that way, even if today I am in the service of the Church."

The humility shining through these words caused a few moments of emotional silence and then a new outbreak of acclamation.

Pius XII, born in Rome, knew his fellow citizens well; he never tried to change them. From the beginning he let them do as they pleased. And in the end, John XXIII was forced to do the same. A comment by Pius XII is illuminating in this connection. When he served as papal nuncio in Berlin he was asked one day by a northerner accustomed to strict church discipline why the Romans behaved in church as if they were in the theater. The reply was swift and witty: "For the same reason that Germans behave in the theater as if they were in church."

WINE TASTING

One fine day in autumn the Pope took a walk in the Vatican gardens. He was in a good mood and was pleased to see at a distance his devoted gardener, who had also come from Venice. The Pope used to talk to him regularly about plants and flowers, and this subject was very dear to him. He was thoroughly familiar with the soil, for he had learned to know it in the difficult role of a farm laborer. Even in his earliest boyhood he had helped out in his father's vineyard at Sotto il Monte.

The papal gardener was about to bottle the 1959 produce from the Vatican vineyards. He quickly filled a small glass with the new wine and handed it to the Pope with the deep bow customary among the peasants. With an understanding look the Pope first raised the glass to the sun, testing its color. The clear sparkling gold confirmed its origin. John then held the glass before him and knowingly assessed its bouquet. He inhaled the aroma of a perfect, sun-ripened fruit, subtly aromatic as the result of the union between a sloping terrain and Riesling vines. Next the Pope fingered the glass to test the liquid for the proper temperature. Only then did he take his first deep swallow, slowly and thoughtfully. He did not open his eyes until he put the glass down. Then he gave a barely audible smack and delivered a typically Roncallian word of praise: "Enrico, do me the favor of not allowing any of the priests who come here to taste this wine. The Monsignors will all want to have it for their Masses, and then they might want to say Mass four or five times a day!"

ZEAL

Ancient, weather-beaten oaks flank the path in the higher part of the Vatican gardens where Pope Pius XII liked to stroll. Nearby stands a fine marble bench surrounded by dense foliage and shaded by a protecting crown of trees. John XXIII liked to go to this refreshing spot, designed in the Italian style of the sixteenth century. Not far away is a miniature grotto of Lourdes sent by French Catholics to Leo XIII for the Vatican gardens. One day John XXIII was accompanied to this inviting bench by an eminent Canadian visitor. To break an uncomfortably long silence, the visitor suddenly asked: "Holy Father, how many men actually work at the Vatican?"

Not inclined to pursue a conversation at the time, Papa Roncalli merely replied, "Half of them."

HIERARCHICAL RANK

John XXIII's first Secretary of State was the temperamental Roman cardinal Domenico Tardini. He was a man who enjoyed speaking in the colorful Roman dialect, even to unknown visitors. It was a way of relaxing the otherwise stiff atmosphere with which he usually surrounded himself like a wall. He was an eccentric, in the sense that he did things in his own way, not in the sense that he assumed odd behavior. A perfect example of his independent attitude was his response to an invitation from the Foreign Press Association, *la Stampa Estera*. They wanted to hold a reception in his honor. He refused to attend unless the money which would have been spent on food and drinks was given to him in cash. He sent it to a Roman orphanage which he had founded. The amount totaled 100,000 lire ($160.00). The newspapermen had to provide their own whisky and canapés.

A true Roman, Tardini delighted in lively discussions. He would contradict anyone. As a student and a seminarian he had constantly challenged his teachers. He feared no one, and he preserved this fearless attitude throughout his life. As an important official in the Roman Curia, he never forbade the men under him to repeat his remarks or the stories which he told. In fact he was delighted if these frequently striking and imaginative statements were spread around. He merely demanded that their origin and content be reported correctly. He required silence only when state secrets were involved.

For many years he had worked with Pius XII, whom he always called "Holy Father." It was very difficult for Tardini to accustom himself to the new style of John XXIII's pontificate. Whenever the new Pope sent for him, his feeling of strangeness led him into the habit of saying, "The one up there is calling me again, just when I have so much to do."

The Secretariat of State is on the ground floor of the Vatican palace, while the papal apartments are on the fourth floor. Tardini continued to use the expression until one day when Pope John spoke to him about it. After an important conversation on church policy, John took his trusted Secretary of State aside. *"Caro Tardini,* I should like to straighten you out on one point. 'The one up there' is the Lord of all of us, the eternal Father in heaven. . . . I am merely 'the one on the fourth floor.' "

There was a pause, then a final thrust: "Please, I beg you not to keep throwing confusion in the ranks!"

NIGHT WATCH

John XXIII did not keep any regular schedule. He improvised and would allow no fixed time-scheme to interfere with his own discretion. Very often this meant that he would not get a full night's sleep. During the first few nights he spent in the papal apartments, the coming and going of the watch outside his door disturbed his nocturnal paper work. Two members of the guards marched back and forth carrying heavy sabers and wearing high boots with clanking spurs. John XXIII considered this procedure merely an expensive form of display.

Finally, as John worked late one night, his annoyance at the noise of the measured strides outside his door was intensified by the coughing of one of the guards, and he decided to intervene.

Just as the two guards greeted each other at a halt, the Pope opened the door. Both men began to snap out their reports according to regulations. "Gently, gently," said the Pope, calming them down. "You don't need to get so excited. It would be better for you both to be home in bed. Better to go to sleep. You don't need to watch over me; I'm protected by the Holy Spirit."

The guards obeyed promptly, turning around to leave. But the Pope called them back and pressed a little box into the hand of the man nearer to him: "And here are a few pills for your cough. Good night!"

ALARM

The papal study was filled with rattling and banging noises. Hammer blows pounded on the ceiling above, and the irritating screech of a handsaw made the din almost unbearable.

Pope John sat at his desk, unable to concentrate. He was aware that renovations were taking place on the floor above, but the workers were supposed to adjust their work, whenever possible, to his frequently lengthy hours away from the study. A shift in the time of one of his appointments must have been to blame for their working now, in the mistaken belief that the Pope was out.

He decided immediately to stop the noise in person. Pius XII would have sent his bodyguard or perhaps Mother Pasqualina, his housekeeper. John preferred to straighten things out himself. Nobody observed him as he left the study at a lively pace.

As soon as he arrived upstairs he realized the difficulty. The workers were putting new planks in the floor, which also happened to be the ceiling of his study. Well, no matter. The apostolic palace had lasted all these centuries because it had been regularly and systematically repaired.

The workers were so surprised at the Pope's sudden appearance among them that they dropped their tools. "Well, since I see how it is," they heard him say, "you had better go on working. Otherwise the palace might fall apart. But perhaps it is not absolutely necessary to hammer directly over my head. Now, I am not blaming you. Each one must do the work he has to do. You have yours and I have mine." After he had talked briefly with each one of them, the Pope blessed the eight men and returned downstairs.

In his antechamber he met an excited group of gesturing officials. They fell to their knees with looks of relief when they saw the Pope enter. An alarm had been sounded because of the Pope's disappearance. Inside his study he found more people with worried faces, including his secretary and even the Vatican police.

"Who are you looking for?" asked the Pope. "Me?" he inquired calmly, pointing at himself with his right forefinger. "It's not worth all the trouble," he informed them. "I was just on the floor above with the masons and carpenters. What you should do is hurry and get a few bottles of wine to take to those hard-working men upstairs. The dust up there must give them a real thirst."

SUPERSTITION

Pope John XXIII restored many traditions which his predecessors had abolished or which had fallen into disuse. For example, even though the Vatican palace is well heated, he wore the *camauro*, or red velvet warming-cap with fur trim, which had originated in the Middle Ages.

There was one custom, however, which Pope John wished to suppress. This was the tradition of giving the white papal skullcap, also called a tonsure cap, to anyone who cared to give the Pope another. Pius XII had often changed skullcaps as many as a hundred times in one mass audience. John's aversion to the custom appears to have stemmed from a visit to Lourdes. He had been sent by Pius XII as his legate to the dedication of a new underground basilica, and he had at that time given his cardinal's cap to the guardians of the grotto. It has since been shown to pilgrims at Lourdes as a special treasure.

Years later, when the mother of a sick child gave him a white skullcap during one of his visits to the *Bambino Gesu* hospital, he put it on immediately and thanked her, without giving her one in return. He consoled the mother by explaining that he wanted very much to abolish the custom. "It borders on superstition. And besides, I don't want to be responsible for making an entire hat factory work just for me."

EXCHANGE OF CAPS

John gave away his red cardinal's cap for the second and last time in the conclave of the Sacred College of Cardinals which made him Pope. This time he was not, of course, supporting superstition, but reinstating an ancient tradition which had been abandoned by Pius XI and Pius XII. In the conclave, just after a pope has been elected, has accepted the nomination, and has announced the name he has chosen, the secretary of the conclave approaches the newly elected pope and offers him the white papal cap. It is the first outward sign of his new dignity. He assumes the fullness of his powers and exercises them from the moment in which he accepts the nomination, even though he is still robed in cardinal red.

Tradition dictates that when the new pope accepts the white cap, he should place his red one on the head of the secretary of the conclave, thereby indicating his intention of making him a cardinal. This means that he would be the first cardinal created by the new pope, and his elevation would be accomplished even before the pope called a consistory.

The exchange of caps signifies a radical transformation in the lives of the two men concerned, but it is also a deeply moving experience for all the cardinals who take part in the conclave. One can easily imagine the excitement felt by Msgr. Arborio Mella, for example, when he handed the white cap to Achille Ratti after the cardinal had chosen the name of Pius XI. But Pius XI was not fond of this particular tradition. Mella knelt before the new pope for a few tortured seconds, then braved himself to look up. Pius XI had calmly placed the white hat on his head with his left hand, and with his right hand he had pushed the red cap deep into the pocket of his soutane. Mella had bowed his head so long in vain.

The newly elected Cardinal Roncalli placed his red hat on the head of the secretary of the conclave, Msgr. Alberto di

Jorio, the only non-cardinal permitted in the Sistine Chapel during the conclave. Doubtfully Di Jorio felt his head. "Yes," said Angelo Roncalli. "I really mean it. You're wearing my cap."

HUMILITY

John XXIII paid considerable thought to all the problems which faced him. He gave his closest attention to every task or request, no matter how small. More than ever before in his life, John felt the responsibility that had been placed upon him in his position as pope. He did not feel it as a burden, as he often assured those around him, but more as a God-given mission, which he therefore carried out joyfully. For this reason John could surmount almost all difficulties with ease. His goodness used to turn opponents into repentant followers. He could never understand how men who held high office in the Church could complain about the burden of their pastoral and official tasks. Once a man is called by the Holy Spirit to be a priest, he used to say, he must assume the responsibility to preach and to practice the love of one's neighbor.

In the first private audience he had been granted, a newly appointed bishop complained to John XXIII that the added burden of his new office prevented him from sleeping. "Oh," said John compassionately, "the very same thing happened to me in the first few weeks of my pontificate, but then one day my guardian angel appeared to me in a daydream and whispered: 'Giovanni, don't take yourself so seriously.' And ever since then I've been able to sleep."

CARNIVAL

In February 1963, John XXIII spoke to the faithful in St. Peter's about the Lenten liturgy. Several thousand people from all over the world listened thoughtfully, but only those who understood Italian could follow the Pope's words. The others had to be content with translations which, necessarily, were condensed versions of the Pope's address. Thus they heard only the essence of the talk and missed the typically Roncallian admonition at the end: "Naturally you can celebrate the carnival. But you should always observe the bounds of moderation, and no one can break the laws of God. If understood in this way, having a good time at carnival is no sin."

THE DIFFERENCE

One of John XXIII's most frequent table companions was Cardinal Testa of Bergamo. One day while they were eating, he told his old friend about a cardinal who wanted to know nothing more about the outside world once he had been elected pope. He even disavowed his relatives, because they no longer seemed distinguished enough.

"That must have been a long time ago," interrupted John. "Anyway," continued Cardinal Testa, "when he entered the bronze doors of the Vatican, he left a swarm of relatives behind him. They tried without success to get the attention of 'their Pope' when he was first carried on the papal sedan chair. They waved and signaled, they shouted the loudest of all, but he took no notice of them. The Pope blessed everyone without distinction, and he gave no indication whatsoever of special affection for his relatives."

John had been listening with a serious expression, but at this point he spoke abruptly: "Don't tell me any more about that, dear Gustavo. It is true that I live on this side of those doors, but I left my heart on the other side."

I AND THE POPE

A worthy Augustinian father used to serve the Pope too assiduously when he offered Mass in his private chapel. It bothered John a little to be assisted so devotedly by this man, and one fine morning he explained his feeling to the eager helper. "Beginning tomorrow, please assist me just as simply as you would any other celebrant. And if any high official reproaches you, just say: 'I and the Pope have agreed on it.' "

DRIVE-IN

While he was at Lourdes to consecrate the new underground basilica, the papal legate had been given a jeep draped with red damask to use as he pleased. The ceremonies called for the bishop to go around the church three times before entering the main gate for the act of consecration. After each circumnavigation he had to deliver a precisely formulated speech.

Partly because of the enormous dimensions of the basilica, and partly because he might be tired, Cardinal Roncalli was permitted to take the prescribed trips in the jeep. When he descended at last at the main door, he whispered to a reporter, "It's a good thing we've left the jeep and can walk now. Otherwise I would have turned this church into what the Americans call a drive-in."

SKILL

As papal nuncio in Paris, Msgr. Roncalli was once unable to avoid a conversation with Maurice Thorez, leader of the French Communists. After the first few polite exchanges, Thorez cleverly maneuvered the conversation to the problem of the worker-priests. He wanted an unqualified opinion from the Papal Nuncio so that he would have a hint as to the Holy See's attitude toward this French phenomenon of priests who lived and worked under the same conditions as their poor parishioners. The Nuncio interrupted him even more cleverly by raising his glass to deliver a toast to French wine. M. Thorez knew very well that Msgr. Roncalli had come from a poor family of vintners and that he was such an expert in assessing wines that his praise would be worth hearing. "Certainly, certainly," Thorez hastened to agree, thinking he would soon return to the subject Thorez had introduced. But this was not to be. The Nuncio lectured him in such detailed academic fashion on the qualities of French wines that he could only listen. After a while the Nuncio left the Communist leader without having given him a single hint of his attitude toward the worker-priests.

CHIVALRY

At another time in Paris, Msgr. Roncalli once attended a banquet where, because of his diplomatic rank, he was seated on the right of his hostess. She was the wife of a South American ambassador. Anyone who did not know it already, discovered on this evening that it was impossible to embarrass Msgr. Roncalli. The attractive hostess wore a beautiful low-cut Dior gown. Because of her companion at the table, her décolleté was not quite appropriate. The dress gave her well-developed figure every opportunity to be admired.

The company at the table felt slightly ill at ease. The guests shot small anxious looks at the Papal Nuncio. No real conversation developed. Not until the entrée was served did His Excellency Roncalli break through the painful silence, to the great relief of those at the table, especially the lady of the house. With vigorous good humor he commented: "I can't imagine why all the guests keep looking at me, a poor old sinner, when my neighbor, our charming hostess, is so much younger and more attractive."

BAPTISM OF AIR

Angelo Roncalli frequently traveled by plane, and obviously enjoyed flying. In March 1958, about seven months before his election as Pope, he made his tenth long flight, from Venice to Lourdes. All the French—bishops, notables, and the faithful —had requested that the Patriarch of Venice, who had served as nuncio in Paris for eight years (1945-1952), be sent as the papal legate to consecrate the newly constructed underground basilica at Lourdes. Since they would be satisfied with no one else, Pius XII could not ignore the request, and he sent the Venetian Patriarch to represent him at the ceremonies.

A Caravelle had been sent to Patriarch Roncalli from France especially for the trip, when that famous plane was still very new. Accompanying him on the flight was a distinguished group led by Msgr. Angelo Dell'Acqua of the papal Secretariat of State. The only journalist permitted to travel with the party was John Passetti-Huntington, who covered the trip for the French and Italian radio networks.

When they were roughly over Marseilles, the reporter put his microphone before Patriarch Roncalli—a recording of the interview still exists. Asked for his impression of the flight in the new machine, the Cardinal made the following reply: "I'm an old habitué of air travel. In my lifetime I've flown further than Lindbergh. The only thing bad about flying for me is that I have to go down again among the sinners on earth, and must interrupt the trips which bring me closer to Paradise."

After this observation Cardinal Roncalli looked around and noticed that a high church official, upset by the flight, had been forced to resort to the use of the paper bag provided for such emergencies. In the best of spirits, the legate departed from his religious-philosophical theme and murmured to Passetti: "I would advise you not to interview some of my colleagues. They have no time for it, because they are undergoing their baptism of air."

MANNERS

An encounter between Nuncio Roncalli and the President of
the Municipal Council of Paris, Pierre de Gaulle, brother of
the President of France, was at one time the talk of all Parisian
social circles. It testifies to the papal diplomat's tact and wisdom. Just before an election, the French clergy had announced
that, of all the parties in France, the Popular Republicans were
closest to the aspirations of the Church of France. The high
ecclesiastical authorities had ignored the fact that de Gaulle's
party, too, claimed to be Catholic. Irritated by this decision,
the President of the Municipal Council was inclined to be annoyed with Rome. The Nuncio learned this when he appeared
at a celebration in honor of the two-thousand-year anniversary
of the city of Paris. Pierre de Gaulle asked him if the presence
of the papal nuncio meant that the Church had revised its position, and now considered the Gaullist party as Catholic, too?
Nuncio Roncalli appeared not to understand and was silent.

Later, as part of the same celebration, there was an exhibi-
tion of old manuscripts and books. Nuncio Roncalli continued
to stand before one bookrack so long that Pierre de Gaulle
walked over to him, hoping to get a response to his earlier
question. Instead, Roncalli seized the book at which he had
been looking and laughingly showed it to the President of the
Municipal Council. It was a book by Gasparino da Barsizza, an
Italian Humanist of the fifteenth century, which had been
printed in Paris. "Here, take it," said Roncalli. "This book was
written by a Bergamese, a compatriot of mine. He discusses
good manners. You ought to read it."

QUICK-WITTED

At a reception in the presidential palace in Paris, Nuncio Roncalli happened to be placed on the left of the Russian Ambassador. While the President greeted his diplomatic guests, the Russian Ambassador whispered mischievously to the Nuncio: "Well, does this mean that even the Vatican is taking a leftist position?"

The Nuncio replied quickly with a broad smile: "Yes, they've placed me on the left here so that I can move you all over to the right—I mean, of course, onto the right path!"

DIPLOMACY

Sometimes it was almost impossible for the members of the diplomatic corps in Paris to get a clear "yes" or "no" from Nuncio Roncalli. His diplomatic sense was proverbial, and it was his conviction that he should not reflect his own opinions, but rather the decisions of the Holy See. Always on his guard against leading questions from his colleagues, he often gave ambiguous, sibylline answers even to questions which appeared quite harmless or were merely light chatter.

Once again Nuncio Roncalli was attending a state reception at the Élysée Palace as one of the guests of honor. The splendid windows were opened wide because of the warmth of the summer evening. After all the official greetings, some guests strolled out on the main balcony, which afforded a really fine view of Paris. The City of Lights appeared at its best, and the guests responded with spontaneous bursts of admiration. The sun had not quite set; the first lights had begun to shine. The Nuncio stood quietly among the illustrious guests listening to one exclamation after another: *"O magnifique! C'est merveilleux! Quelle vue!"* Suddenly a distinguished gentleman approached Roncalli in a friendly attitude, and with obvious sincerity asked him in Italian, "Isn't it splendid, isn't it marvelous, Your Excellency?"

Constantly on his guard, His Excellency replied: "There are people who find this panorama very pleasing."

RESPECT

One day Nuncio Roncalli met the Chief Rabbi of Paris and used the occasion to show him his respect. It was at a diplomatic reception which included the heads of all the different religious communities in Paris. In a long conversation which followed between the two, they discovered that they had many things in common, especially in terms of their human sympathies. When they were finally summoned to dinner they suddenly found themselves—still talking to each other with great interest and animation—standing side by side directly in front of the entrance to the dining hall. Nuncio Roncalli did not permit the ridiculous game of "After you; no, after you" to drag on. He gently steered the Chief Rabbi before him, saying: "The Old Testament before the New!"

TIES

Nuncio Roncalli had invited a few Italian friends and several French priests to a dinner at his home in Paris in honor of his three brothers. It was the first time his brothers had been outside of Italy, and under no circumstances would they stay in the luxurious hotel where their brother Angelo had reserved rooms for them. They felt ill at ease in the lavish surroundings of the hotel and much preferred to be on the upper floor of the Nuncio's more Spartan dwelling, protected by their brother, who was far more experienced in worldly affairs than they. They had had new suits made for this dinner by a tailor in Sotto il Monte, and the bill for the suits as well as for the trip was paid by their brother in Paris.

The time had come to serve the apéritifs, but the Nuncio could not ask anyone to sit at the table because his brothers had not come down. He called up to them, but still they did not come. With an anxious countenance, the master of the house climbed the stairs to find out for himself what was causing the delay. What he saw made him laugh. In one of the guest rooms, all three brothers were standing in front of the mirror, hopelessly trying to knot their ties. They had been torturing themselves like this with no success for almost an hour. "What's the matter with you? Why don't you come down?" he asked them.

"Here, look, Angelo, all our lives our wives have tied them for us. We can't do it. We should have brought at least one of them with us." Laughing, the Nuncio took hold of the tie on the brother nearest to him and fixed it into an elegant knot. He swiftly performed the same miracle on the other two.

All four Roncalli brothers descended the stairs with happy smiles to join the company. After they had been cordially greeted, the three winegrowers tried to explain why they were so late, but they were interrupted in this effort by their brother:

"Now don't make up stories, brothers, just tell them that you're not capable of living without your wives." Then Msgr. Roncalli explained to his guests, "I had to play the part of a wife for all three of my brothers."

DOCUMENTATION

In the first few months after the liberation of France by de Gaulle and the Allied troops, Nuncio Roncalli was asked by the French government to have the Vatican relieve thirty-three bishops and archbishops of their duties because they had collaborated with the Germans. The Communists demanded that eighty-seven ecclesiastical dignitaries be guillotined. Roncalli's sense of justice demanded that great care be taken to examine the actual facts. As the result of an exhaustive ten-months'-long examination of the evidence, only three bishops were relieved of their posts.

Nuncio Roncalli was stubborn enough to give no credence to mere talk. French accusers had actually tried to convince him merely by laying on the table before him a large stack of newspapers which contained shocking stories about priestly collaborators. Without giving them a second glance, Roncalli dismissed them with a single sweep of his hand and said to the French authorities, "These are only newspaper clippings. Please, bring me genuine documents."

GOOD-BY

It was only when His Excellency Roncalli left Paris and the office of papal nuncio that the high esteem in which he had been held there became evident. He had earned it by his vision, his diplomatic skill, his flexibility, his pointed and delightful sense of humor, and his warmhearted human goodness. French President Vincent Auriol, who had given him his cardinal's biretta, had to wipe away his tears with his handkerchief when Nuncio Roncalli left to assume his new dignity as a cardinal.

The representative of the Holy See said good-by in simple words: "It would make me happy if all Frenchmen would look upon my departure as that of a peace-loving priest and a sincere friend. As far as the future is concerned," continued Cardinal Roncalli, "it would be better to say 'au revoir' and not 'adieu,' for the good Lord will surely let me come again *to visit Him . . . in France.*"

WINDOWS

With one exception, the entrance of the new Patriarch of
Venice on March 16, 1953, was marked by an unusually warm
reception by the inhabitants of the city. When the procession
reached the town hall, Cardinal Roncalli noticed to his surprise
that the windows of that official building were closed in an obviously unfriendly gesture which was in marked contrast to
the open windows of the townspeople. He knew the Venetians
and their city well from earlier visits, and had learned to
value them highly. Therefore, he was surprised, and asked for
an explanation. An embarrassed official explained to the Patriarch that the city council was run by Communists, who had
chosen to ignore the Cardinal's arrival. Undisturbed, Roncalli replied, "We shall see to it that these windows open
again."

BEND, DON'T BREAK

Great joy and satisfaction were evident in Venice when Cardinal Roncalli was named Patriarch of Venice. He was reputed to rule with a mild hand. He was also said to be very tactful, charitable, and especially devoted to the poor.

The Venetians had just endured two authoritarian patriarchs. Even while mourning their "Serenissima," Patriarch Agostini, the clergy found themselves unmoved emotionally because of the strict rule he had maintained. He and his predecessor, Cardinal Piazza, had been particularly anxious to eliminate the relaxed moral atmosphere in the Lido, where the international film festivals were held. They placed part of the blame for this situation on the lower ranks of the clergy. These priests felt that they had been unjustly accused, and they were especially happy on this account to have a new Patriarch who was understanding and progressive in his views.

When Cardinal Piazza was nominated to be a member of the Curia, the priests in Venice voiced their sentiments in the remark: "At last that one is going." Piazza, who was not unaware of the joy caused by his approaching departure, warned the Venetian clergy: "You will miss me yet. My successor is inexorable and will lead you with an iron rule." His prediction about Cardinal Agostini proved quite true.

But Patriarch Roncalli did not disappoint the Venetians. Soon after his arrival he told them that his motto was: "Bend, don't break."

GIFTS

Patriarch Roncalli often traveled on the canals of Venice. And just as frequently he wandered through the narrow city streets in order to be in constant contact with the faithful. He wore the clothes of a simple priest when he went out, with no sign whatsoever of his high office. He loved to talk to people, and he was happy to be approached, both by those who knew him and by those who did not. His favorite conversationalists were the gondoliers. He would walk over to them where they gathered in groups to wait for customers. He was a churchman who understood the language of the people.

Occasionally he would also meet priests while he was taking these walks. If he happened to meet one who was unshaven, Roncalli would make it his business to find out the priest's address, and the next day he would send him his calling card with friendly greetings—and a razor. Once he stopped a young priest whose collar was far from white. "My dear vicar," said the smiling Patriarch cheerfully, "I have at home a whole dozen snow-white collars which have become too tight for me. If you would permit me, I should like to make you a present of them."

KIDNAPPER

Corrado Pallenberg tells an amusing story which testifies both to the gracious hospitality of Angelo Roncalli and to the special respect he had for Stefan Cardinal Wyszynski, the Primate of Poland. It happened in Venice. Many distinguished visitors from France, including President Vincent Auriol and Cardinal Feltin, had already visited the former Nuncio, and on each of these occasions Roncalli had seen to it that the "Marseillaise" was played in St. Mark's Square by the municipal orchestra.

Patriarch Roncalli did not want to miss the chance to greet the Polish Primate, who was on his way to Rome for his first trip in many years. His train was to stop at the Mestre station for three-quarters of an hour, and Roncalli invited the Cardinal to take a boat ride during the interval. Wyszynski was enthusiastic in his appreciation of the Grand Canal. He didn't notice the time at all. Suddenly he looked at his watch and cried out, "My goodness; my train—my train has gone!"

Roncalli soothed his visitor in a truly patriarchal way. A mischievous glint appeared in his eyes. "Don't worry! Look over there. That man in the motorboat behind us is the station-master at Mestre. I have kidnapped him. As long as he's here with us, the train *can't* leave."

Even when he was Patriarch Roncalli, Cardinal of Venice, Pope John XXIII offered the Communists no grounds on which to criticize him. Habitual anti-clerical insults gave way to respectful silence. Confusion reigned in the Communist ranks. Roncalli tripled the number of parishes and made gradual but steady efforts so that in a short time the churches were crowded when Mass was offered. Film festivals? Communists? They both had their own limited sphere of influence, but Sunday Mass was being restored to its old honorable position. This was the attitude of the Patriarch.

Even today the Communists are not certain whether they are grateful or hostile to the Roman Pontiff for whom the word "hate" seemed not to exist. They exploited some of his initiatives for their own purposes, but certainly never imagined that he was one of them. The opinion they held of Roncalli while he was Patriarch of Venice appeared in the pro-Communist Roman evening paper *Paese Sera,* and it has not changed since. "Cardinal Roncalli uses his sovereignty moderately and tactfully, but this does not change the fact that he is an absolute monarch in his patriarchate. There is no doubt, however, that he is an open-minded and tolerant monarch."

Western circles were probably just as confused by the Pope's attitude, although their reasons differed, and they seemed incapable of filling in the vacuum which John XXIII created among anti-Christian groups when he lessened their hostility to Christianity. Instead of recognizing the positive advances that had been made in favor of freedom of thought, some even accused the Pope of making advances to Communism. In fact, he contributed heavily to the democratization of the socialist left, which, until 1957, had maintained very strong ties with the Communists, and had even formed a Popular Front with them at one time.

Of course, the inevitable tension between the socialist left and the Communists was greatly intensified by the suppression of the Hungarian uprising. But the "aristocratic peasant" on the Chair of Peter could read the minds of the workingmen of the socialist left far better than Western statesmen. Those Italians who had political sense and were financially well-to-do thought that the Patriarch's appeal to the socialists was a dangerous experiment. But to the workers of moderate inclination, who were undecided and not yet committed to radical views, his appeal was the most natural thing in the world.

The Patriarch had notices placed on the walls all over Venice for the opening of the thirty-second Congress of the Socialist Party of Italy (PSI) in February, 1957. They read as follows: "I welcome the exceptional significance of this event, which is so important for the future of our country. I should like to believe that the decisive motive for your assembly is to understand contemporary conditions and to devote yourselves to doing everything possible to improve living conditions and social well-being." Cardinal Roncalli continued by encouraging all believers and all the inhabitants of Venice to "meet together with their many brothers from other parts of Italy," who share "the ideals of truth, welfare, justice and of peace, in order to develop them as ideas and to shape them into as fruitful a reality as possible." In answer to the anxious question of a journalist who visited him during the PSI Congress, Patriarch Roncalli replied: "Don't be disturbed by my initiative. One day all those people I addressed will come to church again, too."

FIRST REACTION

Those who want to know the character of Pope John XXIII better might be interested to hear his first reaction to the news, told to him in Paris, that Pius XII had named him a cardinal.

"Oh, good heavens," called out the Nuncio. "After this difficult diplomatic post, I would have liked to have been a pastor somewhere, or perhaps a bishop in a diocese in Bergamo. And now—what will happen to me?"

Nuncio Roncalli had no suspicion of the fact that Pius had chosen him to be the new Patriarch of Venice, something he had never dared hope for. Instead, he envisioned himself already as a cardinal in the Curia, head of a Vatican department: "I'll come to a bad end. I'll suffocate in dusty documents or sink in bureaucratic mire . . ."

LEGAL LOOPHOLES

During the period between the death of Pius XII and his own election to the pontificate, Patriarch Roncalli discovered the ability of cardinals who might become pope to profit from loopholes in the law. An Italian proverb says: *Fatta la legge, trovato l'inganno* ("As soon as a law is passed, ways of getting around it can be found"). According to canon law, all the decisions taken within the College of Cardinals before the election of a pope are null and void. The man who is elected is in no way obliged to abide by conditions which individual cardinals or groups of cardinals might have put to him before they gave him their vote, even if their vote was decisive.

A group of Italian cardinals tried without success before the conclave to find out whether Angelo Roncalli, if he became pope, would make the Archbishop of Milan, Giovanni Battista Montini, his Secretary of State.

As their delegate to Venice, the conservative cardinals had chosen a very young, exceptionally able and intelligent non-Italian Vatican official, who had at one time served Nuncio Roncalli as his secretary. Sticking to his conviction that questions are never indiscreet, but answers may be extremely so, the Patriarch met the difficulty by posing a counterquestion:

"I think it is extremely flattering that their Eminences believe I could be pope. But such a thing is quite improbable. I will never occupy Peter's Chair because I am not suited for it. Tell that to their Eminences. How did the Roman cardinals ever get such an idea? But if in God's unfathomable wisdom, such a thing should happen, it is only then that I would begin to think about the question of who should be Secretary of State. Who ever told their Eminences that I was thinking about Montini for Secretary of State?"

BAKE HOUSE

The province of Bergamo in which John XXIII was born is called "the bake house of the clergy," because it produces more vocations to the priesthood than any other Italian province. The Bergamese consider it a high distinction to be sent to Rome to study theology "in the shadow of the Vatican."

The three younger brothers of Pope John—Saverio, Alfredo, and Giuseppe—were the tourist attraction of Sotto il Monte after Angelo's election. Several hundred reporters were soon among their most eager visitors, until it became too much for the Roncalli family. One group of journalists became especially annoying to the Roncalli clan and to the whole population of Sotto il Monte.

The three brothers were asked by several Italian visitors to show them their wine cellar. They willingly allowed themselves to be photographed among their vats, casks, and bottles. They discovered later to their horror that the visitors were press photographers and that the picture had been sold for a high price to the world press as an exclusive snapshot of daily life in the family of the Pope, placing the Roncalli clan in a distorted light.

Just following John's election, however, a friendly relationship existed with the press. The first journalist to see Alfredo Roncalli after the news was announced heard the gray-haired winegrower give this calm explanation: "It was bound to happen sooner or later, with all the priests that have been baked around here."

THE HAT

At a fatiguing reception in Venice, Patriarch Roncalli held his hat in his hand. He saw no one among the many guests sipping cocktails with whom he was anxious to talk. He waited patiently for fifteen minutes, which he felt was required by politeness, before he could take his leave of the host. Suddenly one of the men who had arranged the party tried to take his hat. He wanted to hang it up in the closet. "No, no, leave it alone," resisted the Patriarch, "you never know how useful it is on many occasions to have your hat in your hand."

RUIN

"I come from a poor family . . ." John often used to open conversations with this remark, especially if the person he was addressing attempted to conceal his own origins and good luck or if he boasted of them openly. Mindful of the tradition of the Church, which pays no attention to a man's origin when it advances him in the priesthood, Pope Roncalli always stressed the equality of men before God. There was no hint of resentment in his voice when he said that his own parents were small winegrowers.

A politician complained to the Pope in a private audience that the election his party had just lost would bring about his ruin. "No, no," the Pope said encouragingly, "don't be discouraged by your opponent's success. There are always ups and downs in politics. There are only three ways a man can be ruined: women, gambling, and . . . farming. My father chose the most boring of the three."

PAPA AND MAMMA

After his election, Angelo Roncalli was so deeply moved that he sat in the Sistine Chapel with his eyes closed for a long time before he was ready to receive the homage of the cardinals. With a jerk of the hand, each cardinal moved the automatic mechanism removing the canopy above his chair. The only canopy left was the one above Roncalli's seat. It was the single visible symbol of his new dignity.

The fifty cardinals present waited in thoughtful silence until the new Pope accepted the nomination. It appeared an eternity to them before the necessary ceremonies were begun: the Pope's acceptance, his choice of a name, his explanation of his choice, and the exchange of caps. In reality, only a few minutes had passed.

After the doors of the conclave were opened and the members of the papal family who were present were permitted to present their congratulations, John confided to a friend: "The long pause after my election? I was so moved, so overcome, that I thought of home. My thoughts returned to Sotto il Monte, to Mamma and Papa. . . . And when they dressed me in the white papal soutane, I remembered the moment when my mother dressed me in white for my first communion."

CAREERS

John XXIII was always glad to grant audiences to soldiers. As his superiors had written in his army record, he had been a "brave soldier" himself. In 1902, Roncalli interruped his theological studies in Rome to enter the 73rd Infantry Regiment in Bergamo as a voluntary recruit. When the troops were demobilized he had attained the rank of corporal. In 1915, he served as a priest with the Ambulance Corps. His first post in the reserve hospital of San' Ambrogio in Milan was followed by a much more difficult assignment to the military hospitals and ambulances of Bergamo. In the course of pursuing these duties the corporal had become Field Chaplain Roncalli.

During a special audience when the Chamberlain read the list of visitors aloud, John caught the familiar name of a General, reminding him of his own military background. Deciding to talk to the General, he asked to have him brought to his private library. This caused much surprise, especially to the General. The gray-haired soldier knelt respectfully before the Pope in order to kiss his ring. He reached out for the hand with the Fisherman's ring, but touched only empty air. Surprised and uncertain, he looked up. He could scarcely believe what he saw: the supreme pontiff stood before him smartly, as only a soldier can, with his hand raised in a military salute. He then broke into completely nonmilitary laughter. Finally he asked the stunned officer, "Don't you remember Roncalli from the Ambulance Corps? The time we met in the field hospital in Bainzizza? Well, in any case, I'm glad your career has been so successful. I've been promoted, too. As you can see, I am now chief of the Catholic Church!"

DISCIPLINE

During the First World War, Sergeant-Major Roncalli of the Ambulance Corps tried to make his gentle expression appear more severe by growing a thick mustache. The soldiers knew, however, that their sergeant was incapable of malice. Besides, they gave him very little opportunity to exercise the rather full powers the Italian army gives to sergeant-majors. There appears to have been only one incident which forced him to imprison an insubordinate soldier in his unit. He did so regretfully.

On the following day all the soldiers had leave to go into town, except for the one who was being punished. "What's the meaning of this?" inquired Sergeant Roncalli in astonishment. "You're still in prison? Why didn't you go out with the others?"

"But, Sergeant," the man replied, "you gave me three days."

"True," replied Roncalli, "but I only meant evenings. In the daytime you can go out."

BERSAGLIERI

During election campaigns, Italians hardly ever play their real national anthem; instead, the bands all play the beloved Bersaglieri march.

The Bersaglieri are famous sharpshooters, the elite of the infantry, which also includes grenadiers, Alpine troops, and other infantry regiments. The Bersaglieri are most noted for the fact that they perform all activities—parading, exercising, and attacking—at double time.

General della Marmora organized these troops in the Sardinian army in 1836, modeling them on the French light infantry. The most striking part of their uniform is the broad-brimmed felt hat with its jaunty cock's feather on top. Without going into their heroic deeds in many wars, the Bersaglieri especially distinguished themselves by their seizure of Rome without a struggle on September 12, 1870. This event marked the end of the Papal States, for Vatican City is not a continuation of the old regime. On the 20th of September, 1870, the Bersaglieri entered the Eternal City through a breach they had made in the wall around it near the Porta Pia, and turned it into the residence of Italian kings and the capital of the Italian nation. An imposing monument stands in the middle of the Piazza before the Porta Pia to commemorate that great day, and the street which goes from the gate up to the Quirinal Palace—once the seat of the popes, then the king's residence, and today the home of the President of the Italian Republic—is called *Via del XX Settembre,* the Street of the Twentieth of September.

An English journalist once remarked after reading the inscription on the Bersaglieri Monument that all of Italy's problems would have been solved if only each government were formed from among the Bersaglieri. The marble inscription reads: *Al Bersagliere non resiste nulla!* ("Nothing can stop a

Bersagliere!") It is certainly true that the stirring melody and the fiery rhythms of their march always make Italian hearts beat faster.

The most patriotic Italians consider the march a second national anthem. Foreigners, too, find it highly exciting, especially if the Bersaglieri themselves march to it.

Pope John XXIII heard the march for the last time at his own request during the national reunion of Bersaglieri reservists and veterans in Rome on March 24, 1963. About thirty thousand reservists and veterans had noisily celebrated their reunion that morning in the Colosseum, and later in a more subdued way by laying a wreath at the tomb of the Unknown Soldiers on the Piazza Venezia. From here they marched in double time to St. Peter's Square, where several Bersaglieri bands had already been given their black feathers. The people affectionately call the Bersaglieri "the black feathers" because they wear these ornaments on their helmets. The cock plumes symbolize the mobility, speed, and trimness of the men who wear them.

The Pope wanted all the bands to play the march together. With incredible precision the Bersaglieri bands played their anthem at least three times, directly under the Pope's windows.

Along with the rest of the crowd, John waited for them to stop. But the band leader was carried away, and did not want to end the spectacle abruptly. During the last few bars of the fourth repetition of the march, the Pope finally addressed the crowd through the powerful loud-speaker; only the Holy Father would have been permitted the interruption.

The playing finally ended, and the Pope spoke: "Your march is magnificent, I know, but now let us pray together a little." The Angelus followed, the prayer of thanksgiving for the incarnation of Christ. Then the Pope spoke again to the crowd, "Sixty-two years ago, I was a recruit myself. When they were ready to assign us, the officers of the Ambulance Corps noticed my slim build, saw that my feet were obviously those

[115]

of a runner, and they agreed that here was a good Bersagliere."

Numerous shouts of *Evviva* interrupted his discourse. An improvised chorus sent up the loud message: "The Pope *is* a Bersagliere! *Evviva!*" As soon as John was able to obtain silence, he quieted the popular enthusiasm based on the belief that he had formerly been a Bersagliere, and which meant that in the future he would be worthily honored in the barracks as "one of their own."

"No, no, instead of sending me to the Bersaglieri they decided to make me a simple guardsman, but that didn't prevent me from being a good soldier."

A SLEEPLESS NIGHT

"You can laugh now. Your house has been completely reno-
vated and you can sleep in peace. That wasn't always true."
With these words, Pope John XXIII began to tell the seminarians at the summer house of the Society for the Propagation
of the Faith in Castel Gandolfo a little incident from his past.
The Pope had traveled from his nearby summer residence to
visit the seminarians.

One night, related the Pope, he had been delayed so long on
a trip to the *Castelli Romani* that he was unable to return to
Rome. He was at that time secretary of a section of the Propagation of the Faith. His one hope was to spend the night in the
summer house at Castel Gandolfo. The only person there, however, was an aged porter who had no key to the locked bed-
rooms. He also had no light.

"Finally, after a long search, I found a small dark room
which had a folding bed but no blankets. It was very cold, so I
lay down with all my clothes on. For a few minutes there was
heavenly quiet. Then, little by little, a noise began, which
slowly grew louder and more frequent. Too tired to investigate,
I dozed half the night in this way without being able to fall
asleep. At last the noise and commotion became too much for
me. I arose, opened the door, and saw to my horror in the early
morning light about half a dozen cats, each one with a squeak-
ing mouse in its jaws.

"I was no longer afraid, but neither was I able to do anything with these intruders. Sleep was impossible, for every time
I lay down, the merry cat-and-mouse game began all over
again."

SPRINTER

On March 2, 1963, the Pope received the reigning stars of the Italian track. They were holding their annual meeting in Rome. Swiftly they fell to their knees in the Pope's presence and rose again easily and gracefully. Their officials were not so fast. This gave John an opening for his speech:

"In my youth I, too, was a swift runner. Just think—as a child I ran eight kilometers every day to school and back. Sixty years ago in Rome I could cover the distance from the center of the city to the Monte Sacro quarter and to the Tre Fontane faster than any of my companions. At that time there were hardly any hackneys in Rome and in the center of the city there was only one path for horses. As a recruit I was later attached to the infantry. But today I'm forced to drive all the time. That's why I'm out of practice, and unfortunately I cannot challenge any of you to a race."

TRAMONTANA

Several thousand shivering members of the faithful waited in St. Peter's Square on January 1, 1963, to receive the Pope's noontime blessing. John XXIII had made a tradition of the custom of blessing the crowd assembled in the Square below from the window of his study at twelve o'clock on Sundays and Holy Days, after they had prayed the Angelus together. People from the country often made long and tedious trips from their homes in order to receive the Pope's blessing just once in St. Peter's Square.

Unusually low temperatures prevailed that winter in the Eternal City. For weeks it had been bitter cold, so that the usually elegant Roman women left all their finery at home and appeared in fur boots and thick woolen clothes, lowering their handsome faces against the icy wind and covering their arms to the elbows in muffs. It was, in fact, so cold that the Romans' favorite drink, *espresso,* had been temporarily supplanted by the northern drink of grog—hot tea with rum.

With chattering teeth and stamping feet the people waited for the Pope. John XXIII could not disappoint all this brave devotion, although his doctor had ordered him not to walk directly in front of an open window when the terrible *tramontana* blew through St. Peter's Square. The Romans dread this northern wind which sweeps down upon their city from the mountains. Icy and cruel, it moves across the eternal masses of snow in the Alpine peaks, crosses the Po Plain, and storms into the defenseless Arno Valley, hurling itself against the Bernini colonnade in front of St. Peter's. On days when the *tramontana* blows, anyone who can, sits indoors by a warm stone oven or goes to one of the innumerable Roman *trattoria* to drink mulled wine.

About fifteen thousand freezing but devoted men and women kept calling for Papa Giovanni until the Pope actually appeared. A glass screen, which came up to his chest, was placed before the window to protect him, but it did not cover his chest or his face.

After the blessing, John, who was a little cold himself, did not speak his usual welcome, but instead spoke hastily into the microphone: "Now hurry, run back home. It's terribly cold today. And if you come back next Sunday, bundle up!"

NEW BEGINNING

Secretary of State Cardinal Domenico Tardini had been ill for a long time. He often begged the Pope to release him from his difficult and highly responsible office so that he could take care of himself. His last request remained unanswered for a long time. To circumvent this silence, Tardini called a press conference at which he publicly announced his retirement. He was promptly summoned to see the Pope, who told him that he very much needed Tardini's "spirit, understanding, and heart" at this particular time. He had to stay in office. The Ecumenical Council, for which he had prepared so carefully, was soon to open, and Tardini's presence was essential. Tardini remained until he died.

Who would succeed him? Many names were suggested in the Vatican, most of them in hypothetical fashion. Cardinal Testa? No, he was out of the question because he came from Bergamo, and the Pope would be accused of nepotism. Cardinal Spellman? No, he was an American. The name of Amleto Cicognani was proposed quite suddenly, a man whose brother was also a cardinal. A high official asked the Pope to consider the fact that Cardinal Amleto Cicognani was too old. He was already seventy-eight, much too advanced an age for such an important position. The Pope should seek a younger man for the post, someone whose energy was not already spent.

"What are you talking about, 'energy spent,' 'too advanced an age'?" said John, himself about fifteen months older than Amleto Cicognani. "Cicognani is much younger than I am. When he was born, I was already going to school!" After a few minutes of silence he continued: "Cicognani could bring the experience he gained in the United States to the apostolic palace. He served the Holy See in Washington for twenty-five years—without a break. And in America, old people become

[121]

young again. It's the only place in the world that has a hospital with a motto over its entrance that says: 'Life begins at eighty.' And we're not eighty yet. *Capito?*"

PANORAMA

Amintore Fanfani, leader of the left wing of the Christian Democratic Party, caused a considerable and heated debate as a result of his action in bringing about a coalition of his party with the Social Democrats and Republicans. The wisdom of uniting with these groups was widely questioned. Catholic politicians had reservations about the concessions demanded by the socialists for their co-operation, but in the end they were prepared to go along with the coalition as long as it was possible.

In the Roman Curia, Cardinal Alfredo Ottaviani was well known as an opponent of this left-centrist experiment in forming a government. A clarifying word was expected from him in his role as director of the Holy Office. The Pope, of course, is its actual head. Ottaviani was asked to approach him and subtly sound him out on the subject. The Holy Office believed that the Pope would not be able to evade the intensive probe of its Secretary. It will be recalled that Pius XII had permitted the Holy Office to publish decrees of excommunication against Communists and extreme Marxists.

During one of his scheduled audiences with Cardinal Ottaviani, John listened thoughtfully to his views for some time. He was aware of the concern in certain Roman political circles about the almost revolutionary development that had occurred between Fanfani and Nenni. Ottaviani was convinced that he had persuaded the Pope to his own position.

Without answering any of his arguments, without the least comment, John suddenly and silently seized the arm of the austere Cardinal, turned him around and piloted him to the library window. Flooded with sunlight, Rome lay at their feet. It was a beautiful sight: Roman ochre blended into azure blue on the horizon. Continuing to hold the Cardinal's arm, after a long silence the Pope spoke: "Look, Your Eminence, what a splendid panorama of Rome one can enjoy from here!"

The audience was over.

PAPAL GREATNESS

It is not historians alone who have differing opinions as to the greatness of a pope. Coachmen do too. On April 22, 1963, John XXIII related to his audience in St. Damasus Hall an experience he had had at the time of Leo XIII's death. At ninety-three, the Roman pontiff lay dying, and at that time Angelo Roncalli, a young seminarian in Rome, went to the Vatican almost daily to inquire about the Pope's condition and to pray for his health. Together with some friends from the seminary, he had hired a cab one day to take them to St. Peter's Square. "In those days you could hire a hackney and go all around the city for a dime.

"The coachman was still the pulse of public opinion at that time. Without much encouragement, the cabbie expressed his opinion freely: 'I think Leo XIII is the greatest pope of all time. When he dies, he will, of course, be replaced, but I will be very surprised if the new one attracts as many pilgrims to Rome. No other pope will ever give us coachmen so much work and so much bread as Leo XIII.' "

Pope John smiled with pleasure as he concluded, "And therein lies the greatness of Leo XIII."

CONFESSION

The same cabdriver, when he had been told by the seminarian, Roncalli, that Leo XIII had already had the last rites of the Church, that he had confessed and received communion, asked in astonishment, "You mean the Pope has to confess, too?"

John told the end of this incident in the popular Roman idiom, spoken by the cabbie, to the great delight of his listeners. Translated, his comment was roughly: "My old man was right. He always used to say to me, 'Nino, why don't you try going to church once in a while?' "

YOUTH

The cardinals in St. Paul's Basilica were still deeply impressed by John's announcement that he intended to call an Ecumenical Council in the near future, when an eighty-year-old cardinal arose and called out to the seventy-seven-year-old Pope: *"Santo Padre,* I will co-operate in your great work; I will stand at your side and work with you toward the success of the Council."

Moved by this first spontaneous reaction—the other cardinals did not commit themselves so quickly—John replied: "Your Eminence, leave this difficult work to us, the youth. The program I envision is so extensive, so unbelievably far-reaching, that it can only be carried out by fresh forces."

FRESH AIR

As soon as the Pope, on January 25, 1959, in St. Paul's Basilica in Rome, announced his intention of calling an Ecumenical Council, there was scarcely any rest in the Curia. Its traditional calm disappeared. The four- to five-hour workday was not lengthened, but the Monsignori had to work more industriously. Anyone who thought that the Council could not begin for at least five years because of the well-known thoroughness of the Curia soon learned better. Pope John made use of public audiences in order to break the Curia's resistance.

"The opinion is often heard," the Pope said during an audience in 1961, "that preparations for the Council will require at least four or five years. This is quite wrong. The Second Vatican Council will open in 1962."

Roman ecclesiastical circles bestirred themselves, and the Pope made his deadline. Only once again did he have to resort to a public talk in order to point up the serious nature of the work of the Council and the fact that delays would not be tolerated. "It is said that this great ecclesiastical assembly will last ten years. This is also wrong. After a long recess during the spring and summer of 1963, it will be concluded by Christmas."

Why did the Curia, at the beginning, so strongly oppose the idea of holding a Council? Besides the serious practical, politico-religious, and theological reasons, there can be no doubt that there was a genuine lack of enthusiasm for the job that had been given them. Why, they asked John soon after his announcement in St. Paul's, call an ecumenical council? What is the point of this mountain of work? Surely no real renewal or major transformation could be achieved in a few months.

John XXIII listened quietly to the officials who besieged him.

After a few minutes, he stood up and with an impassive

countenance walked calmly to the window, opened it wide, and took a deep breath. Then he paused, smiled, and said, "That's why."

Pope John being carried on the *Sedia Gestatoria*.

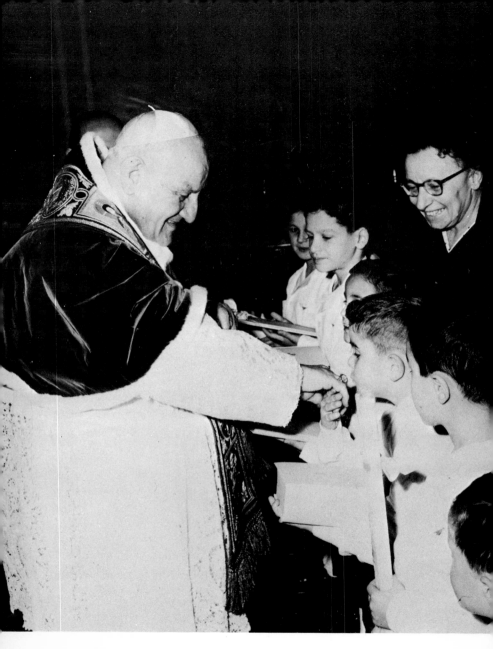

With a group of orphans.

AP

Pope John with Mrs. Jacqueline Kennedy.

A Christmas visit to the Queen of Heaven prison, 1958.

An Easter blessing from the balcony overlooking St. Peter's Square, 1962.

Pope John's cape flares in the breeze as he leaves Santa Maria church in Rome, January, 1963.

A handshake for Cardinal Montini, now Pope Paul VI.

Strolling in the Vatican gardens. In the background is the great cupola
of St. Peter's Basilica.

Already gravely ill, Pope John reads his Easter Message of 1963.

STAGE DIRECTION

The Pope was competent in many areas, but the art of film was not among them. On the night before the opening of the Council, he toured St. Peter's Basilica as an interested spectator. He saw many scaffolds and an enormous number of cables, lights, and cameras. The confusing array greatly interested the Pope, and he questioned the director, Antonio Petrucci, about every detail of the complicated machinery. Petrucci explained at great length that he had been given the honor of making a documentary film on the Second Vatican Council, as the Pope well knew. It would not, of course, all be filmed at one time, but only certain parts, especially the high points of the great gathering of churchmen from all over the world. The Pope listened long and patiently to the director's explanations of the projected film. Finally, he blessed Petrucci and his great project, and, turning around, he said: "Hurry up with your shooting now. I mean, finish up as fast as you can, because the Council Fathers have a lot of work to do, too."

PLANE

When he was asked if he believed that Christians would ever unite, John XXIII answered that he believed they would. The reunion of all Christians must be the ultimate goal of all Christian communities. In the beginning, didn't they all belong to the same Church?

Of course, answered the Anglican visitor who had posed the question, but many centuries have passed since their separation, and the other Christian communities have formed completely separate and firmly established churches of their own. The Catholic Church could not simply ask them to "return." That would not serve as a point of departure for any discussion of reunion, but would, instead, stop any dialogue.

"I realize," said Pope John philosophically, "that it will take a long time. Neither you nor I will be here to celebrate the great feast of reconciliation. Neither will my immediate successors. But someone must begin to clear away the obstacles which stand in the way of the glorious awakening. At any rate, an attempt should be made. If you want to smooth down rough edges, you must first use a plane."

NOVICES

In the course of the Second Vatican Council the first sharp disagreements began to arise between conservative and liberal groups. Worried by the lack of unanimity, several Vatican officials close to the Pope pleaded with him to give the Council a clear direction to follow. But John refused, saying, "It is only natural that every Council Father wants to express his thoughts. That is the holy freedom which the Church respects."

When the worried voices became louder and asked the Pope how on earth things could continue in this way, he gave this answer: "None of us has participated in a Council before. We must let things develop slowly, following their own course. Above all, we must begin by learning. When it comes to a Council, we are all novices."

DEVOTIONS

John XXIII departed from the text of a religious address he was delivering to a general audience on July 6, 1960, to express an opinion which greatly surprised many of the priests present. He suggested that it was not a good thing to increase the number of devotions and cults within the Church. Running around from altar to altar, kneeling before the statue of every saint, and many other new practices which were constantly being reported to him, were, in fact, the product of a superficial and frivolous attitude toward religion. Interior piety clings to traditional practices.

Much later he returned to this theme to treat it in greater detail. In May 1963 he suggested that the life and behavior of St. Peter were as fresh today as ever, and that the faithful could do no better than to take him as their model. Here in the cathedral bearing his name they should think of future plans. "We do not meet here, God knows, to bury tradition and demand new concepts. Let us talk to one another freely, so that there is no need to read between the lines. Let us not deceive ourselves with fairy tales."

ACCELERATOR

After the death of John XXIII, Bernd Nellessen wrote in *Geistige Welt:* "He was one of the most important and most courageous of all popes. He was permeated with a more durable optimism than many who preceded him, and at the same time he was one of the greatest realists ever to occupy the Chair of Peter, an example to all who will follow him. What a pope! If all this rhetoric corresponds to reality, then at the moment when a new pope assumes the white robes of his office, the entire Catholic Church should gather its forces. Pope John has demanded it. If his successor decided to ignore the signal he has given, a wave of depression would pass over the Catholic world. We are not honest if we call someone great, courageous, an example to be followed, and then disobey his wishes. This Pope was great because he was someone who caused great events to occur. The uneasy viewed him with suspicion; reactionaries judged him harshly. If his greatness can be explained in one phrase, it would be that he wanted more than the *status quo.* He took the offensive."

The conductor Robert Craft, a friend and close collaborator of Igor Stravinsky, declared that the famous composer had been more deeply impressed by the death of Pope John XXIII than by any event of recent years. While John was still alive, Stravinsky had begun to compose a Mass which he had dedicated to the Pope—a unique occurrence in musical history.

In a letter to a South-German newspaper, L. Angerbauer of Wessling in upper Bavaria, a Counselor of the provincial court, wrote: "Pope John should have come sooner and lived longer. He awakened the Church from its lethargy for the good of all Christianity. More than any of his predecessors, he left behind him an extremely difficult legacy. He has created the modern image of the papacy."

What did John himself think of his pontificate? He lived

with a clear consciousness of the need for renewal and of Christian unity, but he was willing to leave to others all scholarly commentary on the significance of his term in the papacy. He refused to tax his own vocabulary for this purpose, and he was always aware of his own understanding of his limitations. His opinion of himself was simple: "I'm the Pope who keeps stepping on the accelerator."

DIGNITY

Once when John XXIII was at his summer residence in Castel Gandolfo, he saw and heard a papal policeman rebuked by a superior. The man had not taken a camera away from an especially stubborn tourist, although a clear rule stated that he should have done so. During the special audience that followed, the visitor had "secretly" taken a photograph. The policeman replied to this reprimand by explaining that another man had eventually confiscated the film. No harm had resulted. But this fact was not enough to save him from punishment. He was ordered confined to quarters for one day.

The Pope intervened at this point. He was thoroughly familiar with the security regulations, which he accepted as they were. But he did not like unnecessary strictness, especially not in a case like this where no harm had resulted. "It is easy for a superior to call down a subordinate," he said to the astonished officer, who had not seen him approach. "But always remember that the punishment should fit the crime. To me the punishment seems excessive here, because this is the good man's first mistake. It should be easy to close one's eyes and let him go with a reprimand. But if one raises his voice . . ." Here John pointed his index finger at the officer, a most unusual gesture for him: ". . . whoever shouts is unjust! We must always respect the dignity of the man standing before us, and above all the freedom of every man. God himself gives us this rule!"

PARISH PRIEST

"Holy Father," said a Vatican official of protocol one day to the Pope after one of his trips outside the Vatican, "the Italian authorities responsible for your security are confused because you make so many trips, and you always stop at the red light."

John: "Isn't that the law?"

"Of course, of course, but if they only knew in advance where you were going, and what route you would be taking, because the responsibility is too great, in case something happened."

"Nonsense," said the Pope. "What could happen?"

"Nothing too bad, naturally," the official hastened to reply. "But because of the crowds that assemble all along the edge of the streets, someone might be injured. Traffic has changed since the time of the first John who was pope."

"Oh, well," smiled John, "that will all change. The Romans will soon get just as used to seeing me as they are to seeing a parish priest."

THE VOW

John XXIII was a seasoned traveler. Apart from his own country, Italy, which he knew very well, he had gone all over Europe, to Africa, and to the Near East. In 1912 he visited Germany and Austria for the first time.

He made these visits under orders from Benedict XV to inspect the possibility of greater co-operation between the various countries in mission enterprises. In 1929, now a legate, Roncalli journeyed to Prague, Czestochowa, Warsaw, Posen, Gnesen, and Berlin, where he met Papal Nuncio Pacelli, later to become Pius XII.

It was during a sermon delivered in the Cathedral of Loreto in 1962 that John XXIII revealed the secret which explained why he had been anxious to make this pilgrimage to the sanctuary of the Black Madonna. He had done so in order to annul a sixty-two-year-old vow.

Italian Minister Amintore Fanfani, leader of the Christian Democrats, accompanied him to Loreto, and their mutual sympathy developed into a warm friendship during the trip. Fanfani's hunger for social reform had led him to seek an opening to the left, although the Communists were excluded. And since an opening to the left implies a closing to the right, the parties on the right found themselves excluded. If one is able to find a political attitude in John XXIII's point of view, his policy would seem very close to that followed by Fanfani; he looked at political parties only in terms of their social effects.

The Pope stood before the house in Loreto which is said to be the birthplace of the Blessed Virgin. Pious legends say that angels carried it from Bethlehem far over the Adriatic Sea to Loreto—and it is for this reason that Our Lady of Loreto is the patron saint of aviators. A crowd of several thousand people surrounded John and applauded him as he recalled his first pilgrimage to Loreto sixty-two years earlier. He had been traveling from his home in Sotto il Monte to Rome, to begin his theological studies there. It was on September 20, 1900, the Pope recalled. "The city was draped in Italian flags. The Freemasons were celebrating the day as a victory over the papacy," the Pope said in gentle tones. "I was surprised to see so few people in the Cathedral. No men at all, and only a few old women. After my devotions I wandered on the streets, where my priestly vestments brought forth sneers and ridicule. Some of the remarks made to me were the vilest kind of abuse. I can tell you, I felt miserable. I didn't find it easy to get over these insults, and that same evening I wrote in my diary: 'Dear Lady of Loreto, I truly honor and love you. I will try to serve you, however, as a good seminarian in Rome. I am sorry to have to tell you that you will never see me here again.' "

UNWRITTEN LAW

There are unwritten laws in all areas of individual and public life. During the lifetime of Pius XII, a minor rule had been introduced to the Vatican which came to be known as the Canali Doctrine, after Cardinal Nicola Canali. It stipulated that no one was permitted to enter the Vatican gardens when the Pope took his walks there. Vatican plain-clothes policemen were assigned to stand a few hundred yards away from the pope to see that this rule was observed. The desire of Pius XII and some of his predecessors for privacy was so strong that visitors were even forbidden to climb to the dome of St. Peter's when the Pope was out walking.

John XXIII stopped many of these prohibitions shortly after his ascension to the Chair of Peter. During a walk in the gardens one day, he was advised by a protocol officer that all his movements and motions were being observed from St. Peter's by visitors who were watching him through telescopes from the dome. He ought at least to prevent this intrusion. The Pope replied peremptorily: "Let them look. I'm still worth looking at. Or do you think I might be a cause of scandal?"

PFM

His own stoutness and that of other men was always a favorite theme with John. He would make fun of himself, and even liked to tease "fellow sufferers." He did it with so much charm that the people concerned no longer had any inclination to undertake or continue a program of dieting. "He must increase," the Pope said one day, to an especially slim visitor, a missionary bishop—and then, to complete the paraphrase of his patron saint, John the Baptist, he turned to a far more powerful and corpulent companion of the bishop and concluded, "and he must decrease!"

One afternoon when the heat was oppressive, John XXIII appeared unannounced among the carpenters of the Vatican. The men knelt down as soon as the Pope entered their workroom. It was a long moment before they rose again. The pious expressions on their faces did not disappear until the Pope asked a young worker to fetch two bottles of wine. Glasses appeared instantaneously, and John XXIII drank the good Vatican vintage along with the carpenters. Their shy smiles suddenly turned to joyous laughter, however, when John addressed a remark to a singularly corpulent workman. "I'll bet," said John with a broad smile, "that you're a member of the Party."

The plump carpenter was extremely embarrassed and confused. He struggled with his answer, not knowing what to say. "Holy . . . Holy Father," he stuttered at last, "I'm not in any Party. I don't belong to any political groups."

The Pope slapped the man on the back good-naturedly and said: "There's no need to sign up in the Party I'm thinking of. You become a member automatically. PFM." The carpenter repeated the letters, shaking his head as he did. The other workers mumbled them without understanding, while John enjoyed the puzzled looks on their faces. Then he suddenly blurted out: "Party of Fat Men!"

PARATROOPERS

Among the many groups of soldiers whom Pope John received in the Vatican and in Castel Gandolfo, there was once a contingent of French paratroopers. The Pope praised their courage and said that he had luckily been spared the decision whether to join the infantry or the paratroops because in the First World War there had been no paratroops. The soldiers stood before John straight and full of pride, for they were delighted with the papal praise. Imperceptibly the talk began to turn to spiritual matters. The French paratroopers learned at the end of the Pope's address that he was more concerned about their strict attention to the life of worship than he was with their military prowess. Pope John left them with the thought: "At the same time that you are eager to remember how to come down from the heavens, I should very much like you not to forget how to get back up."

MUSICAL VIENNA

They still remember in Rome today the time the Bruckner Mass in F Minor was played in the Roman Basilica of St. Mary of the Angels, a church designed by Michelangelo. The event was unique from a musical and cultural viewpoint, but was perhaps most significant from an ecclesiastical point of view: It was the first time that a secular orchestra had performed in a Roman basilica. Some members of the Curia, known for their conservative attitude and their indifference to contemporary arts, tried their best to prevent the concert, on the grounds that such a performance, no matter how excellent, did not promote religious ends. Pope Pius insisted otherwise. He not only authorized the performance, he permitted it to be dedicated to him. In the course of events, the president of the Austrian Cultural Institute in Rome, Dr. Egon Hilbert, who had successfully promoted and organized the affair, had occasion to invite six cardinals, many bishops, several members of the Italian government, and many internationally known personalities from the cultural and political world to the Basilica for the performance.

After his coronation, Pope John remembered the notable performance by the Vienna Symphony Orchestra, under the direction of Wolfgang Sawallisch, with soloists Wilma Lipp, Sonja Draksler, Anton Dermota, and Hanns Braun of the Vienna State Opera. He invited Dr. Hilbert to produce a comparable concert in the Vatican. Dr. Hilbert went to great lengths to put on as perfect a performance as possible, and, to show his appreciation, Pope John invited him to a private audience.

In the course of their talk, Pope John discussed an earlier visit he had made to Austria while he had been secretary of the Propagation of the Faith. When he had had an unexpectedly free day in Vienna, he seized the opportunity to become acquainted with the City of Music, and went to a concert hall. He could not recall the numbers that were played, but he had been most disappointed. Much discouraged, he went to the Vienna State Opera and succeeded in getting a ticket in the section reserved for standing room.

This section is a space behind the last row of orchestra seats, where there are long bars on which standing viewers may lean. It represents a praiseworthy tradition in the Viennese theater which does not exist in quite the same form in any other theater in the world. The acoustics and the view of the stage are excellent, and eager young singers and those with little money are able to enjoy the opera very cheaply.

"The young audience viewed me at first with surprise and disapprobation, but then my lively smile must have convinced them that I was enjoying myself, too. Yes, the young people even kept my place during the intermission, although I had left nothing to mark it. And do you know what was playing that day? I really enjoyed myself—it was *Carmen*."

GAY BLADES OF LINZ

To the delighted surprise of John XXIII, the strains of the overture to Rossini's *Tancredi* greeted him as he began an audience on August 6, 1960, at Castel Gandolfo. It was played by the "Gay Blades of Linz," under the direction of Robert Thaller. John immediately asked who they were, and discovered that the men wearing the leather Tyrolean costumes with red jackets were a brass band from Linz that had been hired to play in the Eternal City during the summer Olympics. But first they wanted to play for the Holy Father.

When John read his list of visitors, he gave a special greeting to the Gay Blades of Linz, since he wanted to thank them for their gracious tribute. The band responded to this salute with a triple flourish from all thirty instruments. The audience of almost thirteen thousand people applauded wildly and clamored for more music. The Pope was to choose whatever he wanted to hear.

John XXIII was no spoilsport, and he told the clarinetist, Franz Polak, and the drummer and singer, Walter Heinsich, who were standing nearest to him, "Play a waltz; I never hear Viennese music."

The "Blue Danube" blared out. The Pope was so pleased that he did not give the signal to leave until after the very last bars had been played, and it was amid the jubilation of the crowd that he was carried away on the *Sedia Gestatoria*.

CIRCUS

On December 29, 1958, John entertained a group whose presence caused a considerable amount of disturbance in Vatican City. He gave a special audience to the "Orfei," members of an Italian circus. These traveling artists and acrobats did not come alone; they brought with them their feathered and four-legged friends.

The venerable consistorial hall in the apostolic palace, which had until recently been occupied by the Sacred College of Cardinals, became a circus ring for one performance. The high point of the act was a routine executed by doves. The snow-white artists were not disturbed by the unaccustomed surroundings or by the small size of their audience, but went through their act with bravado, to the Pope's great delight. He applauded them heartily. Most prominent among the members of the circus who did not participate in the performance was a young lion cub just forty-five days old. He seemed right at home in the consistorial hall. He was even more pleased when the Pope tickled his little head and gently stroked his fur. At that point the circus band broke into "Silent Night, Holy Night."

When Pope John thanked these traveling artists for their performance, he also praised them for their faithfulness to an old tradition. He expressed his opinion that it would be a good thing if people entered the edifying world of the circus more often. The Pope took the opportunity to urge parents to take their children to the circus, because there they would lose their fear of wild animals and learn that animals can be friends. Bending down over the lion cub, John said good-by: "Be happy that you have no wings—otherwise I'd keep you here for my coat of arms."

Pope John's coat of arms bore the figure of the winged lion of St. Mark.

A LITTLE BLESSING

March 7, 1963, was an historic day in the Vatican. The Pope received former Italian President Giovanni Gronchi, Senator Armando Angelini, and Professor Arangio Ruiz in the little throne room. They came as official representatives of the Balzan Foundation, whose members had unanimously decided to award its first peace prize, worth about a million Swiss francs, to Pope John XXIII. Besides the members of the Balzan Foundation's prize committee, about a hundred local and foreign newsmen were present at the ceremony.

The foreign journalists were obviously most interested in the Soviet group which was also at the Vatican on that historic day. For the first time, a member of the Supreme Soviet, Aleksei Adzhubei, son-in-law of the Soviet Premier and editor in chief of *Izvestia*, had come to pay his respects to a Roman Catholic pontiff. Beside the imposing figure of Adzhubei, who wore a dark gray suit and a silver gray tie, sat the slim figure of his wife, Rada. She wore a rather light gray costume, but, in keeping with the Vatican custom, her head was covered with a black mantilla.

The day before, Adzhubei had shown himself to be somewhat brash, but on this occasion he seemed genuinely impressed. When he had been asked if his father-in-law would also visit the Pope when he came to Rome, Adzhubei had answered tartly, "At least we know now that the Pope doesn't bite!" Shortly before his conversation with John XXIII, he publicly declared, "As a convinced atheist I am much impressed to encounter such a man of religion."

While the Pope and Senator Gronchi read their speeches, one after the other, the Adzhubeis attentively followed the simultaneous translation which Father Kulik of the Collegium Russicum made for them. Ever curious, Adzhubei asked for the translation of the motto which he saw inscribed on the canopy above the throne: *Ubi Petrus ibi Ecclesia* ("Where Peter Is, There Is the Church"). The exhortations of John XXIII seemed to affect the head of the Soviet press. The Pope never looked directly at Adzhubei, but everyone who was present knew to whom he was primarily addressing his words. It is not impossible that someone in the Kremlin had thought of utilizing Adzhubei's visit in order to test the reality of John XXIII's moves for peace and the conciliatory aspect of his pontificate. People not only seemed to trust this peasant's son on the Chair of Peter, but also to want to make political capital out of him—with interest. But John would not let himself be "used." Instead, he took advantage of this unusual situation to deliver a gentle lecture.

The Pope suggested that, to begin with, every man must observe at least the most elementary rules of good behavior in his social life. He then added that those who wanted peace would have to pray for it and learn to live it in their own lives—in the family, in society, and in international relations. "These are the difficult and well-known duties which enable men to be sufficiently disciplined so that they can temper the exercise of their own rights in such a way as to respect the rights of all those around them, and preserve a civilized tone, whether they are defending themselves against accusations or defending the sacred heritage of the human personality, the family, or the community to which they belong."

The foreign correspondents were politely led out of the audience in the throne room after the Pope's talk. Adzhubei and his group remained behind; it included two Soviet diplomats and the journalists Leonid Kolossow and Aleksei Krassikow, as well as Leon Kapalet, General Secretary of the Soviet-Italian Society in Moscow. Only Adzhubei and his wife Rada were led into the papal apartments along with the Pope's translator, Father Kulik.

The historic conversation of a Pope with a high-ranking Soviet dignitary lasted for eighteen minutes. Monsignor Capovilla revealed something of John's discourse shortly after the Pope's death: homely words of apostolic goodness directed to the Adzhubeis, with a special greeting to little Ivan Adzhubei, the Russian namesake of Pope John. But John XXIII never strove "to undermine freedom in order to save the Church," as some critics have charged.

At the conclusion of the general audience, John made a gesture of helplessness, because Secretary Capovilla had signaled that it was time to end. Arms above his head, he said with resignation, "Now you see what freedom the pope has; he gets orders from all sides."

John gave his blessing to all those present, "and to their families at home." While Adzhubei bowed his head, Rada stood quietly at his side. Her expression was thoughtful. Was she thinking of her father in the Kremlin?

John XXIII gave his blessing with a gesture of inimitable kindness. In a disarming voice he said: "That was only a little blessing. Such a little one can't hurt. Receive it as it was intended—and all your relatives at home were included—in a spirit of reconciliation and for the good of your souls. May peace and justice be always with you."

SOCIALIST

It is a tradition of the Holy See to receive the Roman nobility every year in a special audience around Christmas or New Year's. Roncalli's encounter with the aristocratic families of Italy always possessed an unusual flavor, since it meant that the son of poor peasants would give counsel to rich patricians. In fact, the great bulk of Italian wealth is still concentrated in the hands of its small group of Italian noble familes. Prince Alessandro Torlonia, for example, not only heads the list of Roman society, he is also the richest man in the capital. Most of his wealth comes from his estates.

John XXIII used to show his paternal affection for these noble families by inviting their children to accompany them. They were allowed to sit next to the Pope's throne. They could even play with him if they wished; certainly he would never have restrained them. But he continually reminded the adults of their need for a greater sense of social justice, precisely because they were the bearers of such noble and beautiful names, the descendants of outstanding families who had given several famous popes and numerous cardinals to the Church.

In the audience on New Year's Day, 1963, John appealed to the conscience of the aristocrats: "Do not forget! If the good Lord has given you so much money, then He has also given you the task of caring for the poor and the homeless. One day you must render an account of how you have disposed of these riches. Give them today rather than tomorrow, for if you hesitate for even a single day, others may take them from you by force."

A young son of the Prince spoke with conviction to his parents, who were deep in thought as they departed from the Vatican, "I always said Papa Giovanni was a socialist."

LAWYER

During the private audience he had with Pope John XXIII, John J. McCloy heard a story which cast a playful doubt on the presence of lawyers in heaven.

The Pope was aware that McCloy had been U.S. High Commissioner for Germany and that later he had been President of the World Bank, but he was not sure exactly what position he held when he visited the Vatican. He discovered that his visitor was a lawyer by profession.

"Ah, a lawyer!" Turning to Canadian Monsignor Carew, who had accompanied McCloy and was serving as his interpreter, the Pope inquired: "Should we tell him our lawyer story, or would he misunderstand?"

After McCloy had expressly assured him that he would not be offended, John related the following story with obvious enjoyment:

One fine day St. Peter made an inventory of all the inhabitants of heaven and suddenly he came upon several questionable characters. He hesitated, for he was not sure if his usually infallible memory was at fault or if they had entered without his knowledge. After a long time and much consideration, he came to the correct conclusion that these suspicious looking characters had somehow penetrated the heavenly kingdom from the lower regions. His opinion proved to be correct; after a long and careful survey by the heavenly host, a hole was discovered in the barrier between heaven and hell. Peter wanted to clarify the case immediately in a summit conference with Satan.

He had scarcely outlined the problem when the devil wanted to know what proposals he intended to suggest. Peter suggested that this case was quite obviously one of mutual interest. Heaven did not want to be swamped with the souls of the damned, but it was even more obvious that the devil would not like to have the inhabitants of heaven bringing about belated conversions. Arguing in this fashion, Peter brought about the following agreement. He bound himself to keep the barrier between the two kingdoms in good repair for the first year, and Satan was to make necessary repairs in the year after that. They would then alternate years of responsibility for all eternity.

Satan agreed, and a handshake sealed the bargain. But Peter was tormented by an afterthought, and brought out an objection: "I am afraid that I cannot accept your handshake alone. I suggest that we draw up an orderly contract."

"Fine," said the devil, "perfectly agreeable."

As soon as it was drawn up, they both accepted the contents of the legal document. Peter sealed it with his Fisherman's ring, Satan pressed his hoof into the sealing wax, and the legal formalities were complete.

Peter naturally observed his end of the bargain, and during the first year kept the boundary in perfect condition. But during the second year, several more suspicious figures again appeared in heaven. Peter investigated for himself this time. Sure enough, there was another breach in the wall that could only have been due to faulty maintenance on the part of the authorities in the lower regions. Peter went directly to Satan and castigated him in an angry voice, but Satan merely laughed and replied: "So? What are you going to do about it?"

"What am I going to do?" repeated Peter. "You made a contract with me—here it is. You're not going to deny that that's your hoof there, are you? I should have known I couldn't rely on your word, not even signed and sealed. Oh, well, I'll tell you what I'm going to do. I'm going to take this case to the highest court. I'm going to sue."

"Go ahead," responded Satan with complete composure. "Do you think you'll find even one clever lawyer in heaven?"

[151]

MADAME

To receive the First Lady of the United States, Pope John wanted to memorize at least enough English for his opening remarks. The Secretary of State, Cardinal Cicognani, drawing on his vast experience gained during many long years of service in Washington, explained to the Pope that he should address her either as " 'Mrs. Kennedy,' or just 'Madame,' since she is of French origin and has lived in France." Pope John utilized the few minutes before the wife of the American President entered his private library to practice a few times: "Mrs. Kennedy, Madame; Madame, Mrs. Kennedy . . ." But the minute that she crossed his threshold John forgot everything he had learned in joy at her arrival. He went toward her with arms outstretched and cried out, "Jacqueline!"

WARMTH

Visitors often asked John respectfully, but also out of simple curiosity, what his policy in regard to the East actually amounted to. Many of them were not satisfied with his customary answer, that it was not easy to force politicians to modify their opinions. One day in response to a particularly insistent diplomat he replied, quietly but decisively, "As long as I am able, I prefer to be someone who dispenses warmth rather than cold."

RICH

During a "hand-kissing" audience at the apostolic palace, a German priest in an exceptionally well-cut suit stayed beyond the usual time for such interviews, for the simple reason that the Pope's attention had been drawn to this elegant prelate, and he wanted to speak with him for a few more minutes. Obviously well-off, and distinguished in appearance, a priest from a diocese of millionaires, he towered far above John when he arose from his kneeling position. He looked like the noble St. Martin, this time from the land of the "economic miracle," ready once again to share his coat with a poorer man.

In appreciation of the honor which Pope John had shown him, and encouraged by the Pope's smile, he told the Pope how he persuaded his rich parishioners to contribute to the Church. He was never satisfied with small offerings at Mass. He had well-to-do people in his parish who contributed substantial sums to the social work of the Church at home and internationally. "Do you mean that they give large extra donations?" asked the Pope with interest.

"No, Holy Father, just during Mass," the priest explained. "Before the collection I always say, 'When the basket goes around, I don't want to hear any clinking, only rustling!' "

"Really," John interrupted dubiously, "but isn't that a little —crude?"

"Certainly not, Holy Father," replied the priest eagerly. "My little flock finds the reminder very humorous and a definite stimulant."

John shook his head several times after this explanation, still smiling. "Do you know, dear friend," he said finally, "that when poor men *sacrifice* a coin of theirs, that a part of their heart goes into the collection basket with it? . . . That's the reason I would rather hear—clinking."

POOR

A Pope has rarely had as little as did John XXIII in the way of material goods to leave behind him. Earlier he had put together a sum large enough for his family to buy back the house in which he and his brothers were born. Since this purchase, the Pope's relatives had once again been able to live under their own roof. Originally, the house had belonged to the Roncallis, but they had lost it in times of economic difficulty. (John left his pectoral cross to Cardinal König, Archbishop of Vienna, who wears it only on special occasions.)

Although most people strive anxiously for worldly goods, this pope was not interested in such efforts. The Roman physician, Piero Mazzoni, who cared for John until the end—staying by him day and night—learned from the dying man, for example, that a fountain pen was his only tangible possession. "Take it as a sign of my esteem," whispered John to the doctor. "You have done so much for me, and I have nothing here to repay you for all your care and devotion. I have only this pen. Please take it. It's almost new. I've hardly used it."

READY TO TRAVEL

The whole world followed the suffering and death of Pope John XXIII with deep compassion. Millions waited for the daily radio and television reports from the Vatican; newspapers were literally grabbed from stands. Anxious faces could be seen everywhere. Not only Catholics voiced the worried question: Would he recover? This unusual Pope's absorbing concern with peace had evoked a grateful and sympathetic response from people all over the world. Even atheists were moved by the goodness and mercy of John's life and work. Men everywhere seemed to have confidence in this "pastor of the world."

His encyclicals, *Mater et Magistra* and *Pacem in Terris,* and his calling of the Second Vatican Council provide monumental testimony of his life and his reformist pontificate. Someday perhaps a myth will arise about this Pope because of his great efforts to bring peace on earth, based on the rock of love for men. All his life he believed in the essential goodness of men, and worked constantly to help them make this goodness manifest in their lives and works.

During his difficult struggle with illness and death, John XXIII had one brief interruption in his continuous pain and suffering. For one last time, that gleaming spark shone which filled all those near him with joy, and was a reflection of the gladness the Creator had placed at the heart of Angelo Roncalli. Earlier, on several occasions, the Pope had tried to remove the painful or tragic quality in the fears of those who suspected his approaching death. He constantly reminded people that death is God's will and should not be feared. On November 25, 1962, in referring to his eighty-first birthday, he said that he was ready to follow the will of God at any time.

"Every day is a good one to be born on, and every day is a good one to die on."

In a general audience on January 17, 1963, John recalled the sorrowful news dispatches in the world press reporting his illness, and he affirmed that he was "joyously ready." On January 27, he commented on the premature reports that he was near death: "The Pope still lives. And there is no reason to bury him before he dies." On April 22, John spoke to several hundred children in the courtyard of St. Damasus in Vatican City of the death of the ninety-three-year-old Leo XIII: "At last the Pope had to undergo something which comes to all of us, and probably soon to the Pope who stands here before you."

During the last few minutes of clarity preceding his death agony, John looked around the room and marveled at the large number of people assembled. Someone reminded him that people all over the world, of all religions, were praying for him. "The world says that I am dying now," he murmured, "and yet here I am again among you." John thanked all the faithful for their prayers and then spoke to the Dean of the College of Cardinals, Eugene Tisserant, who had been specially summoned, and to all those present, of his burning desire that his successor might continue the Council to its end. "In the very minute when I am returning home," John continued, "I want to thank the sacred college. I feel like a sacrifice on the altar for the Church, for the Council, and for peace. I bless the sacred college." Those standing around him heard him speak quite softly, in an intense but constantly weakening voice: "God's will be done!"

John himself dispelled the oppressive atmosphere of his death chamber. In full consciousness of his condition—the incurable nature of his illness had been known to him for a long time—he tried to cheer the men around him. He did not want his family and his truest and closest co-workers to be sad. Calling on his remaining strength, he tried to smile, while slowly repeating words of consolation to friends and intimate collaborators. His usual lively gestures were only suggested now as he spoke with an almost pleading voice: "Don't worry so much about me. . . . I am ready to take the great journey. My trunks are packed. I can go at any time . . ."